Special Places

for the discerning traveler

In

NORTHERN CALIFORNIA, OREGON

WASHINGTON, BRITISH COLUMBIA

IDAHO AND MONTANA

By
Fred Nystrom and Mardi Murvin Nystrom
with Editorial Assistance by Nancy Hurlow

GRAPHIC ARTS CENTER PUBLISHING COMPANY
PORTLAND, OREGON

ACKNOWLEDGEMENTS

Special thanks go to Marj Hale for all her help and support, Ed Mitchell our "corporate pilot" for volunteering to fly us over the long distances as we did our research, Chad & Tyler Nystrom as they continue to adjust their school vacations in order to accomodate our frequent trips.

Special Credits

Book Design, Catherine Oller, Faine/Oller Productions, Seattle.

Copy Editing, Jennifer Keller

This edition of *Special Places* was created using advanced electronic publishing software and typesetting equipment. Galleys were typeset on a Linotronic 300 Imagesetter at TECHNAPRINT of Issaquah, WA.

Photographic Contributions

— Steve Bly - 194, 210
— Alan Francis - 49, 50, 51
— Tom and Pat Leeson - cover
— Michael McCarry - 57, 58, 59
— Dana Olson - 131, 132, 133
— Doug Plummer - 61, 62, 63, 73, 74, 75, 81, 82, 83, 91, 92, 93, 103, 104, 105, 111, 117, 121, 123, 129, 135, 136, 137, 139, 179, 180, 181, 183, 185, 187, 189, 201, 202, 203, 207, 208, 209
— Michael Seidl - 77, 78, 79, 174, 175, 176, 219, 220, 221, 227, 228, 229
— Richard G. Shaw - 64
— Randy Wells - 94, 142
— Joseph Woods - 39
— Rex Ziak - 89
— Ray Atkeson - 6
— Ted Wiegold - 205

Copyright © MCMLXXXVII
  Graphic Arts Center Publishing Co., Portland, Oregon

ISBN 0-932575-61-7

Library of Congress Number 87-082767

Printed in Japan

INTRODUCTION

Our concept has always been to search out, by personal visits, independently owned lodging, restaurant and specialty operators who maintain a similar high level of quality, service and personal attention to the needs of their guests. While the ambiance of an urban hotel like the Alexis is different than that of a rural bed and breakfast like the Toll House, the level of personal caring and attention to your needs is consistently high. We do not include chain operations or formula restaurants.

In a concerted effort to add only those few really Special Places, we've taken the step of creating a self-monitoring Association consisting of the innkeepers, restaurateurs and specialty operators who were in our prior editions. These people work with us to help select the new places to be added or the hotels and restaurants to be dropped when their quality goes down or there is a change in ownership. This intense, professional peer scrutiny keeps the quality of the Special Places members very high, and it sets this book apart from all others.

The criteria we've established for a member to be added or dropped from the Association is exacting. Current members must ask themselves, "Would I be willing to stay there myself or to recommend this place to one of my guests?" And, "Are the people running the place highly professional in their approach?" Unless the answer to both questions is "Yes," you will not be reading about that place in this book. This double selection process ensures that you have the best travel experience possible.

During my many years with Sunset Magazine, I was always impressed with their consistent approach to presenting truthful, accurate and reliable information. We try to take that same approach and give you a written and photographic representation as close to the real experience as possible. This is the third edition of our book *Special Places*, and we are very pleased to use four-color photos on all properties in this edition. The color gives a much better feel about each of the featured places, and will help you see why we feel each of the places in this book are so special.

We hope you will enjoy these Special Places as much as we have.

Fred and Mardi Nystrom

TABLE OF CONTENTS

Wine Country

Northern California

California is the legendary Golden State because much of its history has been shaped by the eruption of greed known as the Gold Rush. What began as a myth and the Spaniards determination to find a country of gold, followed by the actual discovery of the coveted prize in 1849, resulted in the shaping of an entire state.

The first inhabitants of the state were Native Americans — thousands of small groups with distinct customs and languages. The land around the San Francisco Bay supported more humans than any area of the state. For nearly 1,000 years Indians enjoyed the bounties of the sea and the land, and had a relatively quiet life. The 16th century brought the first Europeans to Alta California, first Sir Francis Drake, then an influx of Spaniards seeking gold to mine and perhaps a few souls to save. The Indian culture was essentially crushed by the Spanish and Anglo oppression. Missions from those early attempts at conversion are still found throughout the state. In the early 1800s, when Mexico declared its independence from Spain, Mexicans settled across the border, lured by the promise of free land and the hope of discovering veins of gold rumored to be deep in the hills. For nearly five decades the *ranchero,* or cattle ranch, was the symbol of the new California, until the gold myth was brought to life and the face of the state took on a different complexion.

During the first three years of the great Gold Rush, more than 200,000 men, plus a few women and children, came across the Sierra Nevada range in one of the greatest mass migrations in history. Gold magic was no more evident than in San Francisco, where the fortune finders came to dispose of their gold, and others came to help them. The heritage of the Gold Rush days is as permanently embedded in California today as the gold was in them thar hills.

When we travel in Northern California, we think of this dramatic history and how it shaped not only the fate of this state, but that of the entire country.

Diverse Regions

The places mentioned in this book are found in four primary areas, each of which is unique. The Wine Country, the North Coast, the Monterey Peninsula and San Francisco are diverse and special in their own way. California's climate lends itself to year-round enjoyment making these areas suitable for off-season travel.

California's Wine Country is internationally acclaimed for its large concentration of wineries and their highly regarded products. Napa Valley, the most popular of the wine regions in the state, is a blend of old wineries and recent upstarts. The area is best known for its Cabernet Sauvignon, Pinot Chardonnay, Sauvignon Blanc and Johannisberg Reisling. Sonoma County is one of the state's oldest wine producing regions and is recognized for its Gewurtrzminer and Zinfandel. Mendocino County is noted for its Chardonnay, Chenin Blanc and Sauvignon Blanc.

The North Coast is a 400-mile ribbon of jagged headlands, wave-sculpted coves and cliffs, and wind-swept cypress clinging to steep hillsides. Small farms and old barns, grazing cows and wandering deer share the rolling grasslands along the coastal highway. It's a coast of communities, where fishing and lumbering are a way of life, and where natives and tourists alike sense the strength and beauty of the Pacific Ocean. The North Coast is a place for long beach walks and quiet retreats, no matter what the season.

San Francisco is an enchanting city which wins visitors allegiance in a matter of minutes. It's a liveable city, and portrays that comfortable sense to the out-of-towner. San Francisco is also a city that pulses with a certain cosmopolitan liveliness. Performing arts and street performers, fine arts and local crafts, ethnic cuisine and local seafood all find room to thrive in San Francisco.

The Monterey Peninsula, universally acclaimed for its natural beauty, is one of California's primary attractions. Breathtaking seascapes, charming towns and an array of recreational activities make this coastal area a much-heralded destination.

National Parks

Northern California, as opposed to its southern sister, is a great outdoor playground where big chunks of land have been set aside for present and future enjoyment. Being in the great outdoors, to most northern Californians, is a way of life, for it is literally outside one's door. Several of the places mentioned in this book are near the state's national and state parks.

Just 10 miles north of San Francisco is a magnificent grove of redwoods, where some trees reach 250 feet in height and the grand old age of nearly 2,000 years. The Muir Woods National Monument, named for the California wilderness explorer, is a 491-acre preserve for these giants— America's oldest living monuments. Mt. Tamalpais, containing some 30 miles of hiking trails, is within the National Monument and affords spectacular views of San Francisco and the Pacific Ocean. For information, call (415) 388-2595.

Forty miles north of San Francisco (via Highway 1) is Point Reyes National Seashore. This 500-acre redwood preserve, dedicated in 1908, embraces tall stands of coast redwoods whose ancestry has been traced back over a 150 million years. For information, call (415) 663-1092.

Humboldt Redwoods State Park, bordering Highway 101 between Garberville and Redcrest, features the famed Avenue of the Giants (i.e. mammoth redwoods). Contact the Redwood Empire Association, (415) 543-8334, for information.

Yosemite National Park, which stretches over 1,189 square miles east of San Francisco, is one of Northern California's premier attractions; one which is best seen off-season. Yosemite claims the largest concentration of the highest falls, including the 2,425-foot Yosemite Falls, in North America. The valley floor, surrounded by sheer vertical walls topped by domes and pinnacles, occupies eight square miles and attracts 90 percent of the tourists to the park. A park operated shuttle bus provides the most efficient transportation around the valley. Elsewhere in the park, wild flower meadows thread through noble trees where birds, deer and bears find refuge.

Border Crossings

The State Department of Food and Agriculture has established inspection stations along all roads entering California from Oregon, Nevada and Mexico. All produce, plant materials and animals are subject to inspection. To avoid delays, do not transport any agricultural products into the state.

Liquor Laws

The legal drinking age in California is 21, for both purchase and consumption of alcoholic beverages. Liquor is sold by the bottle or can in liquor stores and supermarkets. Alcoholic beverages are sold by the drink in most restaurants and bars from 6 a.m. to 2 a.m.

Climate

Northern California enjoys a particularly mild climate. The wet season generally runs from December through February; the dry season is June through October. Other than the occasional winter rain shower, the sun usually shines over Northern California. Temperatures average a pleasant 50° to 70° Fahrenheit. During summer months, the coastal regions are often enveloped in fog, but it tends to clear by afternoon. The state's hot spots are in the Sacramento and San Joaquin valleys, where summer temperatures may reach into the 100s.

Information Sources for Northern California

California Office of Tourism
1121 L Street
Suite 103
Sacramento, CA 95814
Catalogue order desk: (800) 862-2543

NORTH COUNTRY:

Eureka/Humboldt County Convention and Visitors Bureau
1034 Second Street
Eureka, CA 95501
(707) 443-5097, (800) 338-7352 within California

Fort Bragg-Mendocino Coast Chamber of Commerce
332 North Main Street
Fort Bragg, CA 95437
(707) 964-3153

Mendocino County Convention and Visitors Bureau
P.O. Box 224
Ukiah, CA 95482
(707) 462-3091

WINE COUNTRY:

Napa Valley Tourist Bureau
6488 Washington Street
P.O. Box 3240
Yountville, CA 94599
(707) 944-1557

Napa Valley Vintner's Association
900 Meadowood Lane
P.O. Box 141
St. Helena, CA 94574
(707) 963-0148

Sonoma Valley Visitor's Bureau
453 First Street East
Sonoma, CA 95476
(707) 996-1090

Sonoma County Wineries Association
Luther Burbank Center for the Arts
50 Mark West Springs Road
Santa Rosa, CA 95404

Sonoma County Convention and Visitors Bureau
10 Fourth Street
Santa Rosa, CA 95401
(707) 575-1191

MONTEREY/CARMEL:

Monterey Peninsula Visitors and Convention Bureau
P.O. Box 1770
Monterey, CA 93942-1770
(408) 649-1770

Monterey Peninsula Chamber of Commerce
380 Alvarado Street
Monterey, CA 93940
(408) 649-1770

SAN FRANCISCO:

San Francisco Convention and Visitors Bureau
P.O. Box 6977
San Francisco, CA 94101-6977
(415) 974-6900
Walk-in office in Hallidie Plaza, Powell and Market Streets,
(415) 391-2000; 24-hour "What's Happening" line (415) 391-2001.

Selected Northern California Events

January
Annual Crab Feed — Fort Bragg

February
Chinese New Year Celebration — San Francisco

March
Monterey Wine Festival — Monterey

April
Apple Blossom Festival — Sebastopol
Fisherman's Festival — Bodega Bay

May
Rhododendron Show — Fort Bragg
Bay to Breakers Run-World's Largest — San Francisco
Russian River Wine Festival — Healdsburg

June
Montery Pop Festival — Montery
Napa Valley Wine Auction — Napa Valley

July
Napa County Fair — Calistoga
World's Largest Salmon Barbecue — Fort Bragg

August
Sonoma County Fair — Santa Rosa
Concours d'Elegance — Pebble Beach
Wine Showcase and Auction — Sonoma

September
Mendocino County Fair — Boonville
Monterey Jazz Festival — Monterey
Scottish Games — Santa Rosa

October
Columbus Day Celebration — San Francisco
Fleet Week — San Francisco
Yountville Days Parade — Yountville
Classical Concert, Robert Mondavi Winery — Oakville

November
Thanksgiving Fair — Mendocino
Napa Valley Wine Festival — Napa
Christmas Parade and Tree Lighting — Fort Bragg
Country Christmas — Mendocino
"Gifts n' Tyme" Festival — Napa

December
Hometown Christmas Festival — Fort Bragg
Christmas in Calistoga — Calistoga
Classical Concert, Robert Mondavi Winery — Oakville

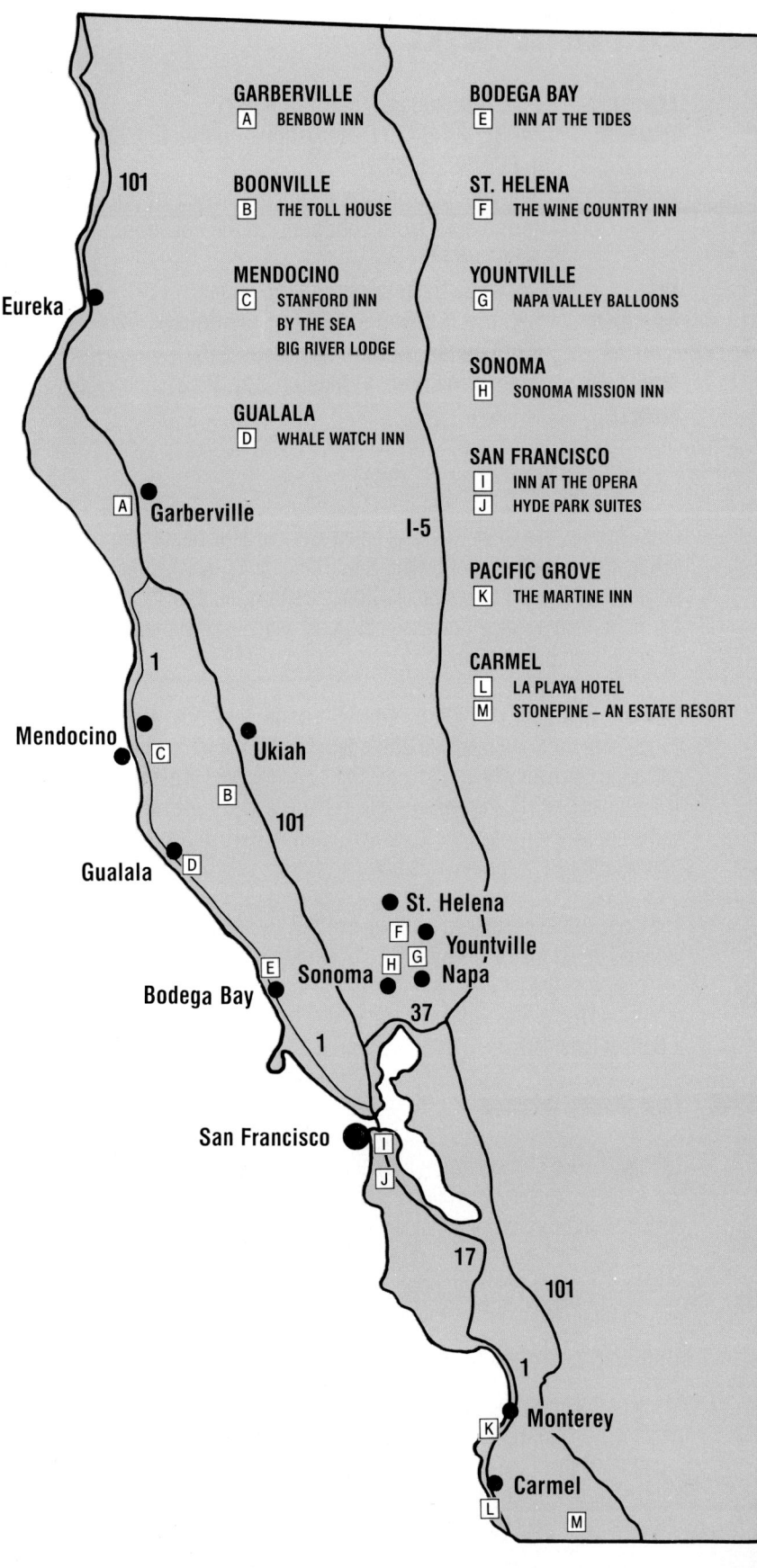

GARBERVILLE
[A] BENBOW INN

BOONVILLE
[B] THE TOLL HOUSE

MENDOCINO
[C] STANFORD INN
BY THE SEA
BIG RIVER LODGE

GUALALA
[D] WHALE WATCH INN

BODEGA BAY
[E] INN AT THE TIDES

ST. HELENA
[F] THE WINE COUNTRY INN

YOUNTVILLE
[G] NAPA VALLEY BALLOONS

SONOMA
[H] SONOMA MISSION INN

SAN FRANCISCO
[I] INN AT THE OPERA
[J] HYDE PARK SUITES

PACIFIC GROVE
[K] THE MARTINE INN

CARMEL
[L] LA PLAYA HOTEL
[M] STONEPINE – AN ESTATE RESORT

101

I-5

Eureka

[A] Garberville

1

Mendocino
[C]

[B]

Ukiah

101

Gualala
[D]

St. Helena
[F]
[H] [G] Yountville
Sonoma [E] Napa

Bodega Bay

37

1

San Francisco [I]
[J]

17

101

1

[K] Monterey

[L] Carmel

[M]

LA PLAYA HOTEL

Address:	P.O. Box 900, Carmel, CA 93921
Telephone:	(408) 624-6476 Reservations, within California 1-800-582-8900
Location:	Two blocks from the beach in Carmel-by-the-Sea, four blocks from shopping, at the corner of Camino Real and 8th.
Host:	Christine Barrett, general manager
Room Rates:	$93 to $150 single, $95 to $150 double, $200 to $325 suites. Additional person $10.
Credit Cards:	American Express, MasterCard, Visa
Remarks:	No pets.

Pretty in pink, this Grand Dame of hotels sits like a Mediterranean villa in the residential hills of Carmel-by-the-Sea. The only full-service resort hotel in Carmel, La Playa is just two blocks from the snowy dunes of the ocean beach. Carmel's main street, a fine assemblage of galleries and shops, is but four cypress-lined blocks away.

La Playa was built in 1904 by artist Christian Jorgensen for his bride, a daughter of the San Francisco Ghirardelli family. The rock work home was a gathering place for writers and artists who congregated in the fledgling town. The sudden death of Jorgensen's wife in 1911 caused him to flee the mansion and eventually sell the home to Agnes Signor in 1916. Agnes added 20 guest rooms, and La Playa Hotel was born.

The Cope family purchased La Playa in 1983. By this time the Grand Dame's wrinkles could not be disguised. Total renovation, intent on preserving her heritage, brought La Playa to her 1985 reopening state. Seventy-five guest rooms and two elegant suites now grace her halls, and the hotel is once again a Carmel landmark.

Four Season Splendor

La Playa's rose-colored exterior is flanked with elaborate formal gardens that are in bloom year-round. Over 3,500 varieties of plants and trees are artfully arranged and carefully maintained.

A heated outdoor swimming pool is set beside terraces with enormous pots of fragrant mixed blooms. A wrought iron gazebo and fountain complete the villa-like atmosphere.

Many of the guest rooms have ocean views, while others look out over the gardens or patio. Hand-carved furniture, with La Playa's Mermaid motif, is found throughout the rooms; tiled showers and a basket of amenities accent the bathrooms. Color televisions are set into carved armoires, and nightly turndown and valet service is provided.

The Mediterranean style lobby is a comfortable place to meet.

The public and guest rooms are decorated with pieces from the Cope family art collection. European antiques and art work, California and Old West memorabilia are everywhere. The lobby's Spanish tiled floor is accented with hand-loomed rugs, and two antique marble figures stand on either side of the fireplace. Conference facilities and a full-time conference coordinator take the strain out of organizing large gatherings.

Spyglass Restaurant

La Playa's dining room, The Spyglass Restaurant, serves breakfast, lunch, dinner and Sunday brunch. The brick terrace beside the restaurant provides an ideal setting for dining while you peer through cypress trees to the Pacific Ocean beyond. Inside, the white linens lend an elegant, old world charm to the small dining room. Personal service is the hallmark of the Spyglass.

Chef Cynthia Kaiser has a high regard for food's nutritional value and designs cuisine to reflect seasonal variations of fresh fruit and vegetables. The Spyglass is known for its table-side presentation. Special dishes for two, including a daily pasta creation, Caesar salad, Châteaubriand and the famous La Playa Paella, are prepared at the table. Rack of lamb Dijonnaise and broiled prawns Veracruz are other house favorites. Flambé desserts, such as Cherries Jubilee, bring an exotic ending to the meal.

Sunday brunch here has gained a reputation of almost legendary proportions. Eight entrées, such as artichoke and bay shrimp frittata or poached salmon with dill Hollandaise, are accompanied by a lavish buffet of pastries, cheeses and fruits. The Spyglass Lounge, decorated in rich wood paneling and Monterey Peninsula artifacts, features a collection of ports and sherries.

The red-roofed inn is two blocks from Carmel's beach.

Quaint Carmel

Fleeing the devastation of the 1906 San Francisco earthquake, writers and artists moved to the hills around Carmel. The site soon became a vacation and retreat spot for city dwellers; but Carmel has maintained a small town sensibility not unlike an 18th century European village. Booksellers, wine merchants, antique stores and art galleries occupy picturesque buildings. At night, couples dine by candlelight in the cozy restaurants. Main street leads to the public beach, where a deli lunch on the sand can be enjoyed.

Along the Coast

Four miles south of Carmel is Point Lobos State Reserve, a 1,276-acre promontory covered with cypress, herds of sea lions and flocks of birds. Further south is Big Sur country, which stretches 94 miles from Carmel to the Hearst Castle at San Simeon. This coastal route offers some of the most dramatic scenery in California. The "Seventeen Mile Drive" departs from Carmel's Ocean Avenue and meanders around the Monterey Peninsula, via the Del Monte Forest, northward toward Pacific Grove and Monterey. Wind-twisted trees and elegant architecture accent the scenery along the way. The Monterery Peninsula has some 17 private and public golf courses, including the famed Pebble Beach.

Getting There

From north or south Highway 1, follow Ocean Avenue into Carmel. Travel west toward the ocean to Camino Real. Turn left on Camino Real and continue to 8th. There is ample free parking around the hotel.

STONEPINE – AN ESTATE RESORT

Address: 150 East Carmel Valley Road, Carmel Valley,
                CA 93924
Telephone: (408) 659-2245
Hosts: Mary Margaret Tate, Director of Sales and Gary Tate,
                General Manager
Room Rates: $125 to $500 double, includes European style
                Continental breakfast
Credit Cards: American Express, MasterCard, Visa, Diners Club
Remarks: No children under 12 in Chateau Noel, however
                children are welcome in the Paddock House.

Stonepine is an elegant estate resort tucked neatly in the folds of Carmel Valley's lush rolling hills. Built for the Crocker banking family in 1930, it was purchased by Noel Irwin-Hentschel and Gordon Hentschel in 1983 and converted into a guest facility. Stonepine combines the grandeur and grace of a country home with the sophistication of a fine resort. On 330 acres, Stonepine is the ultimate retreat for romantics, but also an ideal spot for business or social gatherings.

From the moment you pass through Stonepine's big iron gate, you realize you are somewhere special. The long drive winds through the pine and oak covered grounds past the stables and the Paddock House to the circular drive in front of Chateau Noel. Stonepine's Rolls Royce Phantom V is often parked here, when it's not transporting guests to and from the airport. The grand door is opened by a staff member who whisks the bags away and offers a glass of wine as you get settled. As Mary Margaret Tate, Director of Sales, says, "We want guests to feel as comfortable as if they were in their own country home."

Chateau Noel, the main building on the estate, is lavishly furnished and expertly appointed. The foyer is graced with 19th century limestone columns and a solid oak stairway winding to the second floor. The Library has a marble fireplace, and is lined with French burnished oak paneling, a wedding gift from the Crockers to their daughter and son-in-law. The Library is an excellent place to retreat for a game of chess.

The Living Room is a luxurious, but comfortable gathering place with its grand piano and carved Italian fireplace. Impressive tapestries from 18th century France hang above the mantle. French doors open onto the Loggia, an intimate patio with graceful stone arches supported by ancient Roman columns. The Loggia offers a serene setting for cocktail parties and fireside evenings. A trimmed lawn meets the steps of the Loggia and extends to a rolling meadow. At its edge is a row of 80-foot Italian stonepines.

The Chateau has eight suites, each individually designed and furnished. All are spacious, and feature a jacuzzi tub, remote-controlled cable television,

Chateau Noel's spacious living room leads out into the gardens.

and daily fresh flowers. Each suite was developed around a theme and named accordingly. Guests select from the Taittinger Suite, with marble Roman bath and his and her bathrooms; the Don Quixote, featuring a secluded garden and patio; or the Venetian Suite with canopy king bed and separate entrance. The Chanel Suite is decorated in soft gray satin; the Cartier in warm burgundy tones; Wedgewood in soft blues; the Polo in Hunter green and beige. The Dong Kingman, the smallest of the suites, is decorated in peaches and cream. Four of the suites feature fireplaces. All have king- or queen-size beds (except the Chanel and Wedgewood which have two doubles) and private bathrooms.

The Paddock House is styled after a country ranch house. The four suites in it have a jacuzzi, and the exclusive use of a fully equipped kitchen and dining room. A spacious living room and bar are combined to create the Double H Suite, which features a large fireplace, comfortable sitting area and game table. The large green house has a veranda and a lawn with a small gazebo. Rental of the entire house is perfect for family and business gatherings. Chateau Noel may also be rented in its entirety, or both may be rented at the same time.

Elegant Dining

Dining at Stonepine is an elegant event of the highest caliber. The dining room glows with romantic fire and candle light as guests dine on Limoges and Royal Crown Derby, Waterford and Baccarat. Sterling place settings accent the beautifully set table. Carved oak paneling and a hand-tied Tai'Ping rug add an air of sophistication. Chef Wendy Brodie's innovative fixed price meals consist of four courses, all superb. Special meals to suit any occasion can be prepared in the same fashion by Wendy and her staff.

The West's oldest thoroughbred breeding farm is on the property.

A European breakfast, included in the room rate, is served in the cheery breakfast room or on the Loggia. Light lunches, such as quiche or soup, are available, as are picnic lunches.

Equestrian Center

The Equestrian Center at Stonepine is the oldest thoroughbred breeding farm west of the Mississippi. A team of directors give Western and English lessons, conduct trail rides and carriage driving lessons. A replica of an Abbott Downing stagecoach and haywagon, among other horse-drawn vehicles, are available for romantic rides through the grounds behind a team of Belgian Draft Horses.

Tennis, croquet and archery are among Stonepine's offerings. Future plans include adding a polo and soccer field. A heated pool is located near the tennis court, beautifully set in a grove of orange, lemon and sycamore trees.

The charming town of Carmel-by-the-Sea is just minutes away, where the streets are lined with myriad galleries, shops and restaurants. Nine golf courses are within easy driving distance from Stonepine, including the famous Cypress Point, Pebble Beach and Spyglass courses. Historic Monterey and the beautiful Big Sur coastline make wonderful day trips from here.

Getting There

From Coast Highway 1, head east on Carmel Valley Road about 13 miles. Pass through Carmel Valley to the 13.2 mile marker. The Stonepine driveway will be on your right. Pick up the telephone at the gate for entry.

THE MARTINE INN

Address:	255 Oceanview Boulevard, Pacific Grove, CA 93950
Telephone:	(408) 373-3388
Hosts:	Don and Marion Martine
Room Rates:	$95 to $185 double, includes breakfast
Credit Cards:	MasterCard, Visa, American Express
Remarks:	No children under 16, no pets, smoking in fireplace rooms only.

The Monterey Peninsula spans the rocky coastline beginning just 120 miles south of San Francisco. Its hub is the town of Monterey, a cradle of history for Northern California. native Indians, Spanish conquerors, Mexican ranchers and American settlers have at various times passed through and played their roles in the unfolding plot. Author John Steinbeck depicted the fishing community in his mid-1940's novel "Cannery Row." The area around the original sardine cannery is now a labyrinth of shops, galleries and eateries. Just three blocks from this vital area, where Monterey meets Pacific Grove along the scenic Oceanview Boulevard, is the Martine Inn.

The Martine Inn is a gracious bed and breakfast overlooking Monterey Bay. Built in 1899, the original home was true Victorian. It was owned for many years by the Parke family of Parke Davis Pharmaceuticals, who converted it to a Mediterranean-fashioned villa. The Martine family purchased the home in 1972, and Marion and Don fully renovated it in keeping with the Victorian traditions. "We want our guests to feel as though they are visiting the home as the guests of the Parke's would have at the turn of the century," says Marion.

Complete Suites

In renovating the inn, the Martines took particular care with details. Inlaid oak and mahogany floors were lovingly restored, and the wall coverings and paint carefully selected in keeping with the era. Each of the 19 rooms is individually decorated to reveal a unique character. Elegant museum quality antiques carry out the theme. The Martines have searched extensively for complete bedroom suites for each room, and have unearthed some interesting finds. The Edith Head room contains her own bedroom suite, as well as a commissioned portrait; the McClatchy suite is furnished from the estate of C.K. McClatchy; the Park room features a 1860 Chippendale Revival four poster bed, complete with canopy and side curtains. The Oriental Room boasts an authentic Oriental wedding bed, graced with hand painted panels and beveled glass. The Art Deco room's decor is accented by a lit Coca Cola sign, while the Pewter Room is so in character that even its light fixtures are pewter.

Ocean Views

Thirteen of the rooms have a fireplace. Many have an ocean view, and all have private bath. Two oceanside parlor areas were provided by the Martines, so

This is a perfect room for winter storm watching.

even those without view rooms may enjoy the water vista. An enclosed, landscaped courtyard offers a quiet spot for reading, and there is a conference room available for meetings. Future plans call for a glass enclosed pool room, jacuzzi and steam bath to be added just off the courtyard.

Elegant Service

The oceanside dining room contains an impressive collection of silver and china, all carefully selected by Don and Marion. Most of it is used daily. A 1765 Old Sheffield server, Victorian condiment and pickle service, and signed Tiffany loving cups are but a few of the treasures to be found in the cupboards. Antique china service is used for breakfast, and coffee is served in individual Victorian silver pots.

In the evening, as twilight spreads across the California coast, guests of the Martine Inn gather for hors d'oeuvres and a glass of wine in the parlor. While a fire warms the room, guests sample an array of appetizers from stuffed mushrooms to puff pastry with a proscuitto, honey, and mustard filling.

Breakfast at the Martine Inn is a meal not to be missed. The inn's Italian trained chef prepares fresh and wonderful creations such as crab Benedict, salmon Wellington or Spanish egg bake. Fresh fruit, juice and homemade breads accompany the meal. The full-time chef is available to cater the many weddings, meetings and other functions often held at the inn.

On the Peninsula

The Martine Inn enjoys a prime location on the Monterey Peninsula within easy walking distance of many attractions. In addition to the many shops and

The suites are decorated with authentic antiques.

galleries of the Cannery Row area, the Monterey Aquarium is just a few blocks from the inn. Internationally acclaimed, the aquarium features nearly one hundred innovative habitat galleries and exhibits. Visitors experience Monterey Bay on a journey into its deep reefs and turbulent tide pools. Monterey's historic Fisherman's Wharf houses a large fishing fleet, and it, too, has its share of shops and seafood restaurants. A walking tour of historic Monterey, called the Path of History, winds past the Fisherman's Wharf on its route through the city's important sites. The self-guide tour includes public buildings, ancient adobe structures, and other significant sites where history was made. A map is available from the chamber of commerce. A favorite walk in Pacific Grove is the Victorian tour, which takes you past homes of the 1800s.

The staff at the inn is dedicated to creating a pleasurable, well-rounded experience for the guest. They are able to arrange golf and tennis games, bike rentals, and suggest local dining establishments. The inn's library is stocked with literature on nearby attractions as well as menus from most restaurants.

Some of the finest sites of the Monterey Bay area may be seen from the comfort of the Martine Inn. Winter is the best time to watch for migrating whales, but otters and seals play in the surf, and seabirds feed along the shore right in front of the door year-round.

Getting There

From Highway 1, take the Pacific Grove turnoff. Follow signs on Highway 68 to Pacific Grove. The road becomes Forest Avenue. Stay in the right lane all the way to Ocean View Boulevard. Take a right and proceed 15 blocks to the inn. Private parking is available.

INN AT THE OPERA

Address: 333 Fulton Street, San Francisco CA 94102
Telephone: (415) 863-8400
Host: Annabella Wisniewski, General Manager
Room Rates: $95 to $115 double, suites $125 to $165
Credit Cards: MasterCard, Visa, American Express, Diners Club
Remarks: Children welcome

San Francisco has long been a favorite travel destination. Recently, many of the interesting older hotel and commercial buildings have been remodeled into well furnished alternatives to the large downtown highrise hotels. It is now possible to stay in "the city" and not have to stay in the downtown business core area.

San Francisco is a city of neighborhoods. One of the most vital and creative is the Civic Center, an area rich with the city's major governmental and arts complexes. The cluster of eight buildings around the perimeter of the Civic Center Plaza are said to be the "architecturally grandest in the country." Just one block away is the Inn at the Opera.

Built in 1927 and operated as the Alden Hotel, the Inn at the Opera has a unique history of catering to visiting opera stars, conductors, musicians and upcoming artists. Totally renovated in 1985 under new ownership, the luxury hotel continues to serve many artists and patrons, as well as out-of-town visitors and San Francisco residents.

Full-Service Hotel

Inn at the Opera has 48 rooms on seven floors. Eighteen are suites. Each room features a queen-size bed, fully stocked wet bar and refrigerator, and a microwave oven. Designer wall coverings and matching light pastel fabrics are used throughout. Country armoires house televisions, and plush robes hang in the closets. Original art work, including many performing arts themes, grace the hotel walls.

Inn at the Opera provides excellent, personalized service. Morning newspaper, evening turndown, fine bath toiletries and wake-up calls are just a few of the standard services. The Inn staff attends to personal and business needs, providing meeting rooms and secretarial service, tour and limosine arrangements. They will also obtain tickets to performing arts programs for you.

Future plans for the Inn at the Opera include the addition of 36 one-bedroom suites in the adjoining building. Special function rooms will also be created.

Act IV

Act IV, on the hotel's ground floor, offers gourmet dining. The Act IV lounge is a recognized meeting place for performing artists and patrons, political and

The main lobby gathering area.

civic leaders, and, of course, hotel guests. Rich wood and tapestry walls, thick carpeting and green leathered chairs offer a handsome, intimate setting. While a musician entertains nightly on the grand piano, guests sit by the fire and enjoy a pre- or post-theater drink. The lounge stocks the finest liqueurs available, including a collection of vintage brandies.

Entrées at the Act IV dining room, headed by French chef Christian Janselme, range from medallions of lamb with sherry, garlic and pine nuts to breast of duck in creamy green peppercorn sauce. A vast wine selection pleases any palate. Breakfast and lunch are served in the same classy Act IV style.

In the Center

Inn at the Opera is within easy walking distance of many of San Francisco's attractions. City Hall, considered one of the most beautiful public buildings in the United States, is just one block away. It is a magnificent 1914 structure housing municipal offices, civil and criminal courts that is well worth seeing. Across the plaza is the Public Library, built in 1916, shelving some 1.5 million volumes and several special collections. The 1913 Civic Auditorium, scene of conventions, sports and cultural events, occupies the plaza's south end.

To the west of City Hall is the San Francisco Museum of Modern Art. The permanent collection of 20th century art rotates on a regular basis and includes such masters as Matisse, Klee and Picasso.

The Performing Arts

Inn at the Opera is across the street from the 3,535 seat Opera House. Built in 1932, it is home stage to the San Francisco Opera and the San Francisco

The popular Act IV Lounge is on the ground floor.

Ballet. The Opera is regarded as one of the finest in the country, attracting some of today's foremost artists.

Louise M. Davies Symphony Hall is the lavish home of the San Francisco Symphony. The 1980 built hall greatly increased the city's cultural capacity, permitting longer seasons for the performing arts.

Ten blocks east of the Inn at the Opera is Union Square, hub of San Francisco's downtown, where elegant stores cater to uptown tastes and fashions. The cable car runs from Union Square up Powell Street to Chinatown to the east or Nob Hill to the west. Chinatown is one of the largest Chinese communities this side of Asia, and hops day and night with activity. Nob Hill is the posh crest of the city from which spectacular views of the entire bay area can be seen.

From Union Square, it is an interesting walk down Post Street to the Financial District. En route to the Financial District along Post, one passes the Crocker Galleria, a shopping arcade canopied by a glass vault 70 feet high and 275 feet long. The Financial District is bounded by Kearny Street to the west, Washington Street to the north and Market Street to the Southeast. The most distinctive building in the area is the Transamerica Pyramid, which reaches 853 feet into the sky. The Bank of America, which houses its world headquarters here, is a close second at 778 feet.

Getting There

From the south take Highway 101 north. Exit on Fell/Laguna. Take Laguna to Fulton and turn right. From the north, take Highway 101 south toward Van Ness/Civic Center. Turn right on MacAllister, left on Gough and then left again on Fulton. The hotel is on Fulton between Franklin and Gough.

HYDE PARK SUITES

Address:	2655 Hyde Street, San Francisco, CA 94109
Telephone:	1-800-227-3608 toll free for reservations, (415) 771-0200 for hotel.
Location:	Near Fisherman's Wharf in San Francisco.
Host:	Carlene van Berkel, Manager
Room Rates:	$150 one-bedroom suite, $175 one-bedroom suite with view, $200 two-bedroom suite. Corporate rates available.
Credit Cards:	Visa, MasterCard, Diners Club, Discovery, American Express
Remarks:	No pets.

Surrounded by water on three sides, San Francisco rides the tip of a 32-mile long peninsula. Myriad piers reach like tentacles from its 24-mile waterfront into the bustling bay. One of the most noted waterfront areas is Fisherman's Wharf, a San Francisco landmark, where, it is said, nearly every visitor to the city winds up eventually. For guests of the Hyde Park Suites, this vital area is considered home during their San Francisco stay.

City Suites

The Hyde Park Suites feature three two-bedroom suites, designed to accommodate up to six people, and 21 one-bedroom suites, the result of extensive refurbishing of the building. Many of the suites have a bay view, while others offer a balcony or patio. Each of the suites provides a fully equipped kitchen complete with microwave, dishwasher and quality dishes. A coffee maker is set to perk, with fresh market coffee and teas provided.

Spacious living rooms are furnished with a French country armoire containing a cable television. A comfortable sofa sleeper, original art works, and direct-dial phones add to the homelike atmosphere. Large bedrooms accommodate a queen-size bed and second television set. Plush robes hang in the mirrored closets. Bathrooms include a tub and an array of amenities.

The suites are arranged around a large, open atrium with a lofty skylight where guests meet for a glass of California wine at the nightly hospitality hour. A fountain flowing outside may be heard from the rooms. Flower boxes of camellias and tall fica trees complete the serene setting.

A rooftop terrace, where stunning views of the Golden Gate Bridge, Alcatraz and the Wharf area can be seen, is open for guests to use.

The Hyde Park Suites offers complimentary limosine service to shopping areas, the Financial District or Union Square during the morning hours. In addition, the hotel offers 24-hour concierge service, evening turndown with Ghirardelli chocolates, and a morning newspaper delivered to the suite.

The rooftop deck offers expansive views of the Golden Gate.

Though the hotel is ideally situated near several of San Francisco's finest restaurants, guests may wish to dine in the comfort of their suite. Room service is available from 4 p.m. until midnight. A wide selection of appetizers, salads, sandwiches and desserts is on the menu. Snacks, such as guacamole and tortilla chips or Italian Focaccia bread with salami, cheese and olives, are lighter offerings. Nearly two dozen wines and champagnes are listed, as well as several imported and domestic beers.

Prime Location

The Hyde Park Suites are in a prime location for viewing several of San Francisco's main attractions. The famed 112-year-old cable car system runs directly past the front door of the hotel, offering quick access to many of the city's highlights. The cable cars, which run on cables and pulleys, are the only ones in the world operating steadily as a standard form of transportation.

Within a block is Ghirardelli Square, a three story complex of boutiques, unique shops, bars and restaurants. Built as a woolen mill during the Civil War era, it later became a chocolate factory. Though the chocolate industry has long since moved, a soda fountain in the square sells great quantities of Ghirardelli chocolate, carrying on the tradition in a new way.

Mimes, musicians and street artists line the sidewalks between the Square and The Cannery, just one block away. Once a peach canning factory, The Cannery has gone the same route as Ghirardelli Square and offers a mélange of shops and eateries.

Fisherman's Wharf supports a cluster of seafood restaurants and sidewalk stalls. Authentic San Francisco sourdough bread and chilled crab are typical

All rooms have a fully equipped kitchen.

boardwalk fare. The city is known for its abundance of fresh seafoods, including abalone, shrimp and salmon. The Wharf is home to a fleet of commercial fishing boats, a Scottish-built clipper, the *Balclutha*, and a World War II submarine, the *Pampanito*.

One of the best ways to view San Francisco is via boat. Chartering a sailboat is an option, as is hopping on one of the boats departing from Piers 41 and 45 on regularly scheduled tours of the Bay. The usual route takes passengers along Marina Green, under the Golden Gate Bridge, and returns via Alcatraz and the Bay Bridge. Tiburon is another popular destination, as is Angel Island. The largest island in San Francisco Bay, Angel Island is a 740-acre state park and a haven for hikers and picnickers.

Tours of Alcatraz, the famous island prison, are available from the Wharf area as well. Just over one mile offshore, the island held such notorious prisoners as Al Capone and Machine Gun Kelley. The ruins continue to fascinate visitors, as do tales of the convicts' desparate escape attempts.

The narrow streets of Chinatown are cluttered with goods from herbs to silks. The neighborhood harbors some of the finest Chinese restaurants this side of China. *Dim sum*, a Chinese-style smorgasbord, is a fun dining experience.

Getting There

From the Bay Bridge (Highway 80) take Embarcadero Exit to North Point Street. Turn left and continue to Hyde Street. Hyde Park Suites are on the corner of Hyde and North Point. From the south, follow Highway 101 to the Golden Gate Bridge. The highway becomes Van Ness Avenue. Turn right on North Point to Hyde Street.

SONOMA MISSION INN AND SPA

Address:	P.O. Box 1447, Sonoma, CA 95476
Telephone:	(707) 938-9000, (800) 862-4945 for reservations in California; (800) 358-9022, 358-9027 outside
Location:	18140 Sonoma Highway 12; two miles north of Sonoma
Host:	Peter Henry, General Manager
Room Rates:	$85 to $205 rooms mid-October to April; $120 to $225 rooms April to mid-October. Suites $300 to $475.
Credit Cards:	American Express, Carte Blanche, Diners Club, MasterCard, Visa
Remarks:	No pets. Nonsmoking rooms available.

In a matter of a few years, the Sonoma Mission Inn has blossomed into perhaps the premier luxury health resort in the West, rivaling those with years of established reputation. Located on a sprawling campus of eight acres, the Sonoma Mission Inn is a majestic place complete with old Spanish adobe exterior, towers bearing flags, and a massive courtyard. A circular driveway leads visitors into a vaulted beam ceiling lobby with plush furnishings and a forest of lush indoor plants.

A History of Note

The Sonoma Mission Inn and Spa was built upon a hot springs discovered in 1895. The inn attracted wealthy San Franciscans who came by stagecoach during the gaudy 1890s. The draw was a dip in the tepid waters and a wrap in the medicinal mud from the springs. A fire destroyed the original hotel in 1923, but it was rebuilt in 1927. Over the years, millions of dollars have been spent on improvements and expansions, including the addition of the spa facility in 1981, and 70 new guest rooms and suites in 1986.

Today, Sonoma Mission Inn and Spa has 170 guest rooms, a state-of-the-art spa and two superb restaurants. Co-owner and general manager Peter Henry says, "Our intent is to make this one of the world's classic resorts."

Wine Country Rooms and Suites

Near the center of the grounds are newly completed guest rooms and suites. Each has a marble-faced, wood burning fireplace, balcony and large bathroom. Furnishings are both tasteful and comfortable; the spacious rooms are equipped with AM/FM radio, color television with remote control, individual alarm clocks and robes available for use at the spa. Upon checking in, guests are welcomed with a complimentary bottle of the inn's own Sonoma wine.

Amenities range from complimentary newspapers to babysitting services, from same-day dry cleaning to secretarial or limousine services. The resort also operates the Big 3 Market, which carries food specialty items, wines,

The lobby is the hub for many activities.

sundries and all kinds of picnic supplies. The Big 3 Fountain serves lighter meals in a bistro atmosphere.

Stately Estate

The grounds are all one would expect from a classic resort. Flanked by old bell towers is an entryway arcade which faces a courtyard filled with old oaks, sycamore, eucalyptus and palms. The tile roof and floors and the stucco exterior add their own touch of Spanish charm.

The large lobby, totally renovated in 1986, is where the inn's staff serves fresh fruit, cheese and wine to guests each afternoon. Off the lobby is the Grille Restaurant, which serves Wine Country cuisine (fresh, seasonal and local) and delicious low-calorie Spa cuisine. Food is varied and reasonably priced. A wine cellar stocks more than 275 Sonoma valley wines.

European Style Spa

The star of the show is the spa facility itself. The Grecian-inspired coed bathhouse includes something for everyone: an aerobic studio, sauna, steam room, indoor and outdoor whirlpools, Keiser-Cam II weight rooms and an outdoor exercise pool with hydrostatic weight scale.

A full-time spa director and staff attend to guests' needs, offering full-body and hydro-massages, herbal wraps, guided morning hikes, and an array of beauty treatments including manicures, pedicures, facials, hair and scalp treatments and make-up service. Nutrition consultation is also offered, as are private tennis lessons on one of the resort's two lighted courts. Reservations are recommended for all spa activities and programs.

All rooms come with complimentary bottles of wine and mineral water.

Around Town

The town of Sonoma is precisely two miles from the inn and it is a treat to visit. Site of the last mission built by the Franciscan friars in the early 1800s, modern Sonoma is lined with boutiques in a broad plaza across from the restored Mission San Francisco Solano, now known as the Sonoma Mission.

Just beyond town lie a dozen wineries, each worth the visit and the trip to the tasting room. Famed Buena Vista, known for its superb chardonnay, is just minutes outside the town square.

Twelve miles north of Sonoma the Jack London Historic Park sits upon the land the famed author so loved. In addition to the museum, a one-mile walk along a trail through the woods brings you to the site of the ruins of London's burned-down Wolf House. The author's grave, covered simply with the slab of rock he requested, is two-tenths of a mile from the ruins.

Sonoma County is the cradle of much of California's history. Settled by European immigrants, Spanish missionaries and Mexican soldiers, the area holds a rich and colorful past. Be sure to visit nearby Healdsburg's museum with its impressive display of artifacts from the 1850s.

Getting There

From San Francisco, take U.S. Highway 101 north across the Golden Gate Bridge to Highway 37, continuing to Highway 121, which becomes Sonoma Highway 12 on the outskirts of town. Follow Highway 12 three miles to the Sonoma Mission Inn and Spa, watching for signs on the highway.

NAPA VALLEY BALLOONS, INC.

Address: P.O. Box 2860, Yountville, CA 94599
Telephone: (800) 253-2224 toll free in Northern California, or (707) 253-2224
Room Rates: $145 per person
Credit Cards: Visa, MasterCard, American Express
Remarks: Reservations required.

Napa Valley is a valley for all seasons. Corridors of mustard plants radiate vibrant golden hues in spring, brilliantly lit against the dark wild oaks. Summer's fields are a quilt of earthy wheat browns and grapevine greens. In autumn, the vine's leaves are transformed into a patchwork of colors as rich as the grapes they bear. Amidst the groves of eucalyptus and pine, between the stands of ancient oaks, rest grand chateau wineries.

There are few better ways to experience Napa Valley than via a hot air balloon. The 26-mile long valley is known for its gentle, predictable winds, and most days are ideal for flying. Napa Valley Balloons, Inc. is well equipped to create a safe and memorable flying experience.

Established in 1978 with the launching of a single balloon, the company has expanded their fleet to ten. Eight pilots and a large supportive ground crew comprise the competent staff. Operated by five co-owners, it is the largest company in the valley, carrying about 8,000 passengers annually.

Dawn over Napa Valley

The Napa Valley ballooning experience begins at dawn, before the sun's warmth causes the winds to kick up. Balloons are launched from various sites in the valley, but often they leave from the Domaine Chandon Winery. Acres of lifeless Dacron cover the ground. As the balloon's gaping mouth is shot with flame it begins to rise like a giant awakening from a nap. The wicker gondola is then boarded by six passengers and a pilot, and the colorful, inverted pear balloon lifts gently from the earth.

Climbing to around 1,000 feet, the balloons ride the air currents, gracefully maneuvering through the valley. The elevation is altered by the degree of heat blasted into the balloon. The pilots scan the vista, assessing the winds, continually changing the balloon's altitude to steer by the currents.

When the balloon is ready to set down, about an hour after takeoff, a first-rate chase crew is waiting. On busy days, new passengers board, the ship is refueled, and a second group takes off.

Champagne Celebration

Following the balloon flight, a champagne celebration takes place in a nearby park. A table spread with elaborate trays of cheeses, cold cuts, fresh bread, baskets of fruits, vegetables and dips, and pastries awaits. Champagne and orange juice flow freely as the successful flight is toasted. There's something special about a balloon flight: a certain comraderie develops. Napa Valley Balloon's staff members join in the fun, snapping souvenir photos for participants, singing songs and ceremoniously presenting a balloon replica pin.

Ballooning is a safe sport, and the Napa Valley personnel have a special knack for making the flight seem effortless and light hearted. They have flown with small babies and centenarians alike, and all land with a certain effervescent smile and a special memory of their lofty experience. No special clothing is required, as the air is often warmer aloft than on the ground. The only thing you really need to bring is a camera.

It is recommended that you spend the night prior to your flight in Napa Valley so you will be rested for the early departure. Due to changing weather conditions, it is best to reconfirm your departure time and location the night before, although the final launch decision is not made until sunrise.

Getting There

Yountville may be reached by following Highway 29 north from Napa. Directions to the specific meeting spot will be given upon confirmation of your reservation.

Experience the wine country in a special way.

THE WINE COUNTRY INN

Address:	1152 Lodi Lane, Saint Helena, CA 94574
Telephone:	(707) 963-7077
Hosts:	Jim Smith, Innkeeper and Sheila Ticen, Manager
Room Rates:	$106 to $126 double, $15 for additional person. Rates include Continental breakfast.
Credit Cards:	MasterCard, Visa
Remarks:	No pets, no children under 12.

The Wine Country Inn rests amidst the cultivated vineyards of Napa Valley, a part of California's famous wine producing region. Just as fine vintage wines are wrought of toil, dedication and love, so is this charming country inn.

Family Ties

One of the oldest continually operated inns in the region, the Wine Country Inn began as Ned and Marge Smith's dream. Intent on opening an inn, they traveled extensively on the East Coast to gather ideas. They wanted to recreate the look and character of older inns, yet combine it with the comforts available today. The Smiths engaged the entire family in the creation of their inn — the men to carry out the masonry, building and furniture refinishing, the women to stitch quilts, comforters and pillow slips. The result of their efforts was a three story stone and wood structure which, although completed only a dozen years ago, blends beautifully with the vintage wineries it neighbors.

Country Views

Because of the inn's placement on a knoll, every room offers a country view. Wild mustard, lupines and poppies flourish, and a row of Chinese pistachios line the driveway. Each of the Wine Country Inn's 25 rooms has a slight character trait which sets it apart from the others. Perhaps it's the private balcony, or the large patio edging the lawn. Maybe it's the window alcove, or the hand painted canopy bed, or the Victorian headboard reworked to handle a king-size mattress. Fifteen of the rooms have a free-standing fireplace. The prevailing motif is country; the colors used include blues and whites, reds, rusts and browns. All rooms have a private bathroom, air conditioning, and piped in classical music with individual volume control. The antique furnishings are from various periods; each has been hand selected by the Smiths.

Quiet Nooks

What each of the rooms has in common is comfort. There are no telephones or radios, yet there are plenty of books and quiet reading nooks. There are pastoral views and intimate rooms ideal for romance.

The inn has an outdoor swimming pool with plenty of lounge chairs around it, and a large bubbling spa nearby. Pool towels and robes are provided.

The Common Room is the location for great breakfasts and social gatherings.

Hearty Continental Breakfast

The inn's Common Room is the gathering place for a hearty Continental breakfast served daily from 7:30 to 9:30 a.m. Homemade granola, a variety of breads from zucchini to nut, fresh juice, fruits and coffee comprise the morning meal. Guests can eat around the large refectory table or on the deck. The Common Room is also well stocked with books and games to keep you entertained during other times of the day. Pots of tea water and coffee steam continually. A refrigerator is also available for guests' use.

The Wine Country Inn is not far from over a dozen fine restaurants that serve lunch and dinner. Their menus are stacked on a Common Room table for guests to review, and the staff will be glad to make the phone call to secure a reservation. Now that's hospitality.

The Wine Country

Napa Valley is the largest and most popular of the wine regions in the state. Between the cities of Napa and Calistoga, over 140 wineries dot the valley. Their volume ranges from 500 case cottage wineries to million case producers. The valley evokes a somewhat European air with its miles of vineyards, small farmhouses and great stone wineries. Among the valley's old and great wineries are Beringer, Christian Brothers and Charles Krug. Spring Mountain Vineyard's Miravelle Mansion is noted for its role in the popular television drama *Falcon Crest.* Sterling Vineyards, which is accessible by tram, sits like a monastery on a knoll over the upper valley.

Most wineries in the valley are open to the public and offer tours and tasting, but a few wineries may be visited by appointment only. The Wine Country Inn

The quiet inn is moments from nearby wineries.

staff will provide information on wineries and wine tasting and make appointments for guests as requested.

St. Helena, the wine country's capital, is noted for its 40 wineries and historic buildings. Chic shops, unique restaurants and scenic parks line the main street through town. The Silverado Museum features Robert Louis Stevenson memorabilia, where over 7,000 items recount his life and global adventures.

Yountville, south of St. Helena, is noted for its historic, renovated brick and stone buildings. Vintage 1870 is a maze of small shops and eateries.

Eight miles north of St. Helena is the resort town of Calistoga where mineral and mud baths are provided *de rigueur* for visitors. The Calistoga mud bath begins with a soak in a warm mixture of volcanic ash, peat moss and mineral water. A mineral water bath follows, then sauna, blanket wrap and massage.

Calistoga, Yountville and St. Helena are artist communities, where galleries are filled with local paintings, crafts and photographs.

One of the best ways to view the wine country is via an early morning hot air balloon ride. Bicycling is popular in the valley, and hiking is enjoyed in the surrounding hills.

Getting There

From San Francisco, take the Oakland Bay Bridge to Highway 80, then head northward to the Napa cutoff. Travel Highway 29 through St. Helena, continuing one and three-quarter miles to Lodi Lane. Head east one-quarter mile to the inn, which will be on your left.

INN AT THE TIDES

Address:	P.O. Box 640, Bodega Bay, CA 94923
Telephone:	(707) 875-2751, (800) 541-7788 for reservations within California
Location:	800 Coast Highway #1 on the Sonoma Coast 68 miles north of San Francisco
Host:	Jeff Hoffe, General Manager
Room Rates:	$100 to $175 single/double occupancy during summer season (April to November), $85 to $150 winter rates; $10 for additional person. Multiple night stay, subtract $25 in summer, $10 in winter
Credit Cards:	American Express, MasterCard, Visa
Remarks:	Two night minimum when Saturday included. Children under 12 stay free. No pets.

Stretching nearly 400 miles from San Francisco Bay to the Oregon border, the Northern California coastline conjures up visions of ancient mariners in foul weather skins seeking shelter in a protected harbor. Sheer cliffs, pounding waves and rugged headlands punctuate much of the north coast shoreline. Along this coast is Bodega Bay, where historians conjecture Sir Francis Drake's *Golden Hind* may have made its California landfall in 1579. A traditional fishing village, Bodega Bay is more recently known as the locale for Alfred Hitchcock's spine tingling classic *The Birds.* On six hilltop acres above the bay is The Inn at the Tides, a luxury coastal resort. The Inn at the Tides is as uniquely suited to romantic retreats as it is to corporate functions.

Hilltop Resort

The deluxe resort has 14 wood shingled buildings arranged on landscaped hills. Each of the 88 guest rooms has a view of the bay and the fishing village through its grand windows. The spacious rooms have high, vaulted ceilings; many have skylights. Most of the rooms have a wood burning fireplace. The decor, a mixture of natural oak furnishings, soft rose and earth tones, blends naturally with the surroundings, reflecting the pastoral beauty of the area. Each room has a queen sofa hide-a-bed in addition to the queen, king or twin beds.

All guest rooms are equipped with a refrigerator, telephone, individually controlled thermostat, clock radio, and remote control color television. Complimentary newspaper, firewood delivery, toiletries, terry cloth robe, and room service are among the inn's amenities. Fresh flowers and local artwork add the finishing touch to the decor.

A Pampering Place

Tastefully enclosed by hillside plantings, the outdoor pool extends indoors as well. Heated year-round, the pool is plenty large for swimming laps or just relaxing. The spacious whirlpool spa is ideal for nighttime star gazing. A roomy Finnish sauna is just inside the pool house near the changing rooms, and a therapeutic massage is available by appointment.

Wine Makers dinners are held here each winter.

Bayside Dining

The inn's fine dining room, appropriately named the Bay View Room and Lounge, overlooks the harbor. A complimentary Continental breakfast is served buffet style for inn guests here. A linen-covered table lined with trays of fresh fruits, pitchers of juice, and platters of pastries offers many choices.

Dinners are served Friday through Sunday, from 6 to 10 p.m. Menus change weekly, highlighting a superb selection of local seafood and continental cuisine. The dinners are all five-course meals, featuring a tasty appetizer, soup or salad, a pasta dish and an entrée such as seafood, game hen, beef or pork. Dessert, like the seasonal double chocolate Black Forest Torte, is included in the fixed-price meal. A la carte items are available, as well as a broad selection of local wines.

In winter, the resort is the setting for the acclaimed Dinner with the Wine Makers series, featuring gourmet cuisine and a presentation of the wine making region's finest vintages by the wine makers themselves. The series generally runs from January through April on Thursday nights.

Across Highway 1 is the Tides Restaurant, which specializes in seafood, where Tippi Hedren and Rod Taylor dined in *The Birds*. It is an informal place where boats carrying crab, shrimp and salmon dock to unload their day's catch.

Coastal Wanderings

Guests at the Inn at the Tides are often tempted to curl up by the fire or lounge by the pool and not stray far from the grounds. Those wishing for more activity can find a wide selection within a short distance of the resort. Charter fishing

The pool also has an indoor swimming area.

may be arranged from the wharf area. Strolling the fishing docks gives a firsthand look at the array of fishing, sailing and power boats, and a bit of local color. For golf enthusiasts, Bodega Harbor Golf Links is only one mile away. If you don't golf, the Robert Trent Jones, Jr. designed course is worth the drive just for a look.

A drive out to Bodega Head offers excellent views of crashing surf and jagged rocks. The tidepools here merit exploration, and seals can be seen basking on the rocks. Point Reyes to the south and Fort Ross to the north are both visible on most days. Most of the Sonoma County coast north of Bodega Bay is state beach with comfortable access and dramatic views. Coastal driving is often curvy and slow, particularly on weekends, so allow plenty of time to take advantage of the many vista turnouts.

The small town of Bodega, two miles inland, is home to several century old buildings including a church, schoolhouse and a few homes. An art gallery, post office, tavern and general store comprise the town's business district.

Sonoma Valley wineries are just one-half hour away in the Valley of the Moon. Sonoma is one of the state's oldest wine producing regions, and the first wine area north of San Francisco.

Getting There

From San Francisco, drive north on Highway 101 toward Petaluma. Just before entering Petulama, watch for signs to Bodega Bay and follow Washington Street through town. Join Highway 1 in Tomales and continue northward to Bodega Bay. The Inn at the Tides, on the east side of the highway, is directly across from the fishing pier. From the north, take Highway 1 into Bodega Bay.

WHALE WATCH INN BY THE SEA

Address: 35100 Highway 1, Gualala, CA 95445
Telephone: (707) 884-3667
Hosts: Irene and Enoch Stewart, owners, Beth Bergen Innkeeper Manager
Room Rates: $125 to $195 double. Additional person $20.00. Two-night minimum on weekends. Three-night minimum on holiday weekends
Credit Cards: Visa, MasterCard, American Express
Remarks: Rates include breakfast. Adults only; no pets; smoking on decks only.

The Whale Watch Inn by the Sea is perched 90 feet above the Anchor Bay beach on California's Mendocino Coast. The inn is characterized by its contemporary architecture and spectacular ocean view. Each of the 18 rooms is designed to reflect a particular mood, from Art Deco to French Provincial, and the Stewarts' creativity is evident throughout the decor. Luxury, privacy and personal service are trademarks of the inn.

The inn began nearly two decades ago when Irene and Enoch Stewart moved to the coast, seeking a bit of solitude from city life. The "banana belt" climate coupled with the pure scenic beauty of the area captured their interest. The present inn, comprised of five buildings, resulted from their desire to share the area with others. The Whale Watch Inn was created as a special retreat from the workaday world, where the tranquility of the coast could be fully enjoyed.

Suite Selection

The first-time visitor to the Whale Watch Inn may have difficulty selecting from the melange of rooms. None would be a poor choice, though, as each is designed to offer the best ocean views. Most have a fireplace, whirlpool bath and vaulted ceilings with skylights. Fine linens and thick down comforters cover the queen-size beds. Each room is really a small suite, providing ample room for relaxing. Private decks are ideally suited for sipping wine and listening to the pounding surf.

The Bath Suite and Country French Suite both feature a spiral staircase which leads to the second level. The Bath Suite offers the ultimate bathing experience with its whirlpool set on the second floor under a skylight. The Country French Suite's second floor contains the sitting area and a wet bar; the whirlpool is on the main floor. The Showcase Suite is also elegantly appointed with custom designed Queen Anne furnishings from the Santa Rosa Symphony League Showcase Home. Two private decks and a cozy alcove for the bed make this a most romantic suite. The multi-level Silver Mist features a contemporary Art Deco motif and an elevated two-person whirlpool with a view through the fireplace to the ocean beyond.

The "Silver Mist" Suite is a romantic hideaway.

The 14 other rooms are equally dramatic and unique. Four condominium-type accommodations in the Sea Bounty building offer a fully equipped kitchen, which make them ideal for longer stays. The original Whale Watch building houses two small guest bedrooms. Each has a private entrance, private deck and very close proximity to the ocean.

The large, comfortable community room in the Whale Watch building is dominated by a circular fireplace. Sofas, game tables and easy chairs line the walls. Shelves of novels and stacks of games are available for guests' use. On Saturday evenings, wine and cheese are served here around a cozy fire. With no televisions or phones, the atmosphere offers the utmost in solitude.

Breakfast in Bed

After a deep sleep, guests wake up to breakfast delivered at a pre-arranged time. Fresh baked breads, cheeses, yoghurt and fruit may be on the day's menu along with an egg dish such as quiche or frittata. The white linen and china your meal is served on adds a touch of refinement. Those staying a number of days will find a variety of breakfast items, each beautifully presented.

Coasting Along

A private stairway descends to the beach some 90 feet below the inn. Beach walking and tidepool exploration are year-round events here. November through May is whale watching season. Tennis, golf and horseback riding are not far away, and six miles south of the Whale Watch along Highway 1 is Gualala Point Regional Area, where hiking trails ramble along bluffs and headlands. Beach access and picnic facilities are available.

The "Ocean Mist" Suite has a well supplied fire.

The charming town of Gualala has a number of art, craft and photography galleries. This historic community has a colorful past: Pomo Indians, Russian trappers, Mexican land owners, German settlers and Chinese cooks have all had a hand in settling the area. A selection of fine restaurants is within a short drive of Gualala and the Whale Watch Inn. The inn staff is well acquainted with the area and happy to assist in making reservations.

Point Arena Lighthouse, approximately 15 miles north of Gualala along Highway 1, stands on the point of the U.S. mainland closest to Hawaii. The area is site of countless shipwrecks. First constructed in 1870, the lighthouse stood until 1906 when the lens and tower were destroyed in the great San Francisco earthquake and fire. The rebuilt 115-foot tower has withstood the tests of time and the rigors of nature to this day. A museum at the base chronicles its history, and a tour includes a trip to the top.

Highway 128 runs eastward from the coast into the heart of the Anderson Valley and some of Mendocino's premium wineries. Between Philo and Navarro are a few of the smaller wineries, where visitors have a chance to sample wines and perhaps meet the wine makers directly. The staff a the hotel will be happy to assist with arrangements if needed.

Getting There

Take Highway 101 to Petaluma. Go west through Two Rock and Valley Ford to Bodega Bay. Follow Highway 1 north to the Whale Watch at Anchor Bay, five miles north of Gualala. Or, take Highway 101 to the River Road turnoff, four miles north of Santa Rosa. Go west through Guerneville to Jenner. Follow Highway 1 north to Whale Watch Inn.

THE STANFORD INN BY THE SEA BIG RIVER LODGE

Address: P.O. Box 487, Mendocino, CA 95460
Telephone: (707) 937-5615
Location: At Coast Highway One and Comptche-Ukiah Road in Mendocino
Hosts: Joan and Jeff Stanford, Owners and Innkeepers
Room Rates: $115 to $190, including champagne breakfast
Credit Cards: MasterCard, Visa, Diners Club, American Express, Discover
Remarks: Two-night minimum on weekends. Pets accepted.

The century-old town of Mendocino perches on a broad headland of Northern California's rugged coast. Once a thriving logging and ocean-going community, Mendocino's Victorian buildings are now home to art galleries, handicraft shops and fine boutiques. Mendocino's residents blend the polite reserve of their New England heritage with the casual, artistic flair of California coastal life. The result: an attractive town in a most spectacular setting. Mendocino is one of those rare travel finds that needs to be slowly savored. There are few better ways to appreciate the Mendocino area than from the Big River Lodge.

The Stanford Inn by the Sea (a.k.a. Big River Lodge) rides the shore of the Big River. Backed by a curtain of redwood forests, the inn faces the Pacific Ocean and overlooks Mendocino. Ancient apple trees from the historic China Gardens, lovingly cultivated rows of vegetables and flowers, and verdant lawns flank its hillsides. Ducks and geese paddle around the pond while a family of llamas and a pair of robust Morgans graze nearby.

Joan and Jeff Stanford, former Carmel innkeepers, bought the property in 1981. At that time, a rather non-descript motel occupied the site. The Stanfords created a refined, comfortable country inn to take its place.

Country Charm

"What we wanted to create was a special experience," says Jeff Stanford. "That's why we built a true country inn where guests would feel at home." Each of the Big River Lodge's 25 rooms opens onto a deck, offering panoramic views of the ocean and the grounds. Each has private bathroom stocked with fragrant soaps and lotions. Wood burning stoves and fireplaces add country fashioned warmth. The rooms are tastefully decorated with country floral prints, four poster queen- and king-size beds, authentic antiques and fine reproductions, and natural wood paneling. Plants and books create a homelike atmosphere, while a decanter of local wine on a silver platter adds a pampering touch. The Stanfords have a vast collection of local art which graces the rooms.

Continental breakfast includes champagne.

A small Nantucket style cottage near the river contains two lovely units equipped with full kitchen, separate bedrooms and a sitting room. A couple of miles down the road, the Larkin House accommodates larger groups in its three cozy bedrooms, living room and kitchen. It, too, offers an ocean view and all the Stanford amenities.

After a restful sleep, guests stroll into the cheery lobby to assemble their breakfast tray. Under a copper domed server are warm and delicious sweet rolls, especially designed for the lodge and baked in brick wood-fired ovens. Juice, a basket of fruits, coffee or tea, and chilled champagne complete the meal. Guests may linger in the lobby, or may pick up the daily paper for a leisurely morning on their flower festooned deck. Either way, guests are guaranteed an unhurried start to the day.

Ever upgrading the lodge, the Stanfords have plans for the addition of ten deluxe suites adjacent to the main building, as well as a barn, a dining room, expanded lobby and more extensive gardens.

Catch-A-Canoe

The Big River winds through a forested canyon that opens into Mendocino Bay. Its undeveloped shores are home to a host of wildlife, including deer, black bear, beaver, blue heron and osprey. The first eight miles of the river are gentle tidal waters, ideal for swimming and canoeing. Big River Lodge owns and operates a canoe rental program called Catch-a-Canoe, and their fleet of nearly 40 canoes is available for hourly or day-long excursions on this Class I river. After a brief lesson and a few pointers, canoeists paddle into the wilderness for exploration, photography, fun and relaxation.

The bedrooms all have a fireplace.

Coastal Wanderings

The Northern California coast offers intriguing sights in any season. The windswept shore is often battered by winter storms, which bring in driftwood, shells and other treasures dredged from the sea. A long, beautiful beach is just minutes from the lodge, offering prime strolling, picnicking and sunbathing. Experienced scuba divers may explore the undersea world, while fishing enthusiasts reel in salmon and steelhead.

Big River Lodge loans mountain bikes, the fat-tired version of traditional bikes, for jaunts into Mendocino or along forested backroads. Logging roads lace the hills beyond the lodge where bikers ride among redwoods and firs.

Fort Bragg lies along the coast to the north of Mendocino. As the terminus of the famous "Skunk" railroad, it is an attraction for families and railroad buffs. A round trip on the railroad, which takes about six hours, crosses 31 bridges and trestles as it meanders through the redwoods.

Strolling Mendocino's boardwalk, one discovers nearly 50 galleries and shops. Fine restaurants are found in the town and along the coast, and the staff at Big River Lodge is very helpful in directing guests to the better finds. Van Damme State Park, also near the inn, has interesting pygmy forests, and Mendocino National Forest offers over one million acres of protected land for the outdoor enthusiast.

Getting There

From Highway 1, head east on the Comptche-Ukiah Road just south of Mendocino. The inn is clearly marked on your left.

THE TOLL HOUSE

Address:	15301 Highway 253, P.O. Box 268, Boonville, CA 95415
Telephone:	(707) 895-3630
Host:	Beverly Nesbitt, Owner and Innkeeper
Room Rates:	$60 to $108 double, additional person $15, includes country breakfast
Credit Cards:	Personal and travelers checks preferred. MasterCard and Visa accepted
Remarks:	No young children or pets.

The Toll House country inn sits quietly nestled in the firs of Bell Valley. In the heart of Mendocino County, it is just minutes from internationally recognized wineries, and less than an hour from the magnificent Mendocino Coast. The Toll House is small, lending it a cozy, friendly appeal.

Built in 1912, The Toll House was once headquarters for the Miller Family Ranch, a sheep grazing and hop growing holding. An intermediate owner had begun renovation with the thought of creating a hunting lodge. Former model and seafarer Beverly Nesbitt purchased the property in 1981. "I was walking two feet off the ground the first time I saw the house," she says. "Each room was better than the previous one."

The Captain's Return

Beverly learned that Highway 253, which runs in front of the inn, was once a toll road for tree haulers. Thus it seemed only appropriate to name her inn the Toll House. She redecorated the house with a theme reminiscent of her ocean-going days. "I call it the Sea Captain's Return," Beverly says. "It's the type of place a sea captain would wish to come home to."

The Toll House has five guest rooms, each very distinct. The Library, beautifully appointed in rich greens and burgundy, is oriented for wheel chair access. It is the largest room, featuring a fireplace, private bath, sun porch and a queen-size Murphy bed. A ship's brass nameplate hangs above the fireplace. The Blue Room is tastefully decoated, and has a fireplace and private bath, too. Mollie's and Kathy's rooms, named for one of Beverly's daughters and a granddaughter, are very spacious and share a bath. Mollie's rose, black, blue and rust colors are beautifully coordinated in the wallpaper and fabrics. Kathy's room is a cheery blend of peach and lime. Both contain a queen and twin bed. The Bicycle Shed is a small, barnlike building just behind the main house with two twin brass beds cozily made with plaid flannel linens and scarlet spreads. The bathroom is across the courtyard in the main house.

Tiered wood decks lead from the house to the gardens. A hammock swings lazily under a tree, where guests can lounge with an engaging novel. An inviting hot tub whirls in a nearby wood gazebo.

The inn flanks the old toll road.

Beverly pays special attention to guests' comfort by doing such things as providing a bottle of chilled local wine for them upon arrival and furnishing each room with a diary-like book for guests to share thoughts and stories. These notes are fun to read before snuggling between sheets already warmed by a sheet warmer.

Country Feast

Beverly is an accomplished cook who takes great pride in her hearty country breakfasts. In the pleasant, airy dining room overlooking the gardens, guests dine on one of the daily Toll House specialties: Belgian waffles topped with pure maple syrup, New Zealand bacon and egg pie, and freshly baked breads. Fresh fruits, juice and fresh ground coffee accompany the meal.

Dinner at the inn, a fixed price, multi-course feast prepared and elegantly presented by Beverly, may be arranged with advance reservations. One of the more popular entrées is "Margaret Parducci's Lamb," lamb from the local winery owners' ranch. Guests are welcome to bring their own wine and liquor.

There are a number of restaurants in nearby Boonville, Mendocino and Ukiah. Beverly will gladly assist in making an appropriate selection.

Central Location

The Toll House is in close proximity to a diversity of activities. Mendocino County is a noted wine producing region, with several major wineries within easy driving distance. The Parducci family, who have been making wine in the area for three generations, will take you on an interesting tour.

Private dinners can be arranged.

The small town of Boonville, just four miles from the Toll House, is known for "Bootling," a dialect derived from English, Scotch-Irish and Indian words. It is said that the language was created by the younger generation to confuse adults and outsiders. Many local signs capitalize on its uniqueness, and some residents are fluent.

Anderson Valley extends from the eastern edge of Boonville to the town of Navarro, spanning some of California's most dramatic scenery. It is an area of excellent wines, and many small wineries here are gaining recognition. A drive on Highway 128 is a pleasurable way to spend the day. Bird watching, picnicking, hiking and photographing should be on the agenda along the Navarro River.

The Pacific Coast, with its vintage town Mendocino, is less than an hour from the Toll House. An exceptional array of shops and galleries, as well as fine restaurants and a repertory theater, await in this delightful town. One mile north of town, Russian Gulch State Park is laced with hiking and biking trails through dramatic fern canyons.

Back at the Toll House, Beverly's dogs Raley and No-Name sit quietly on the front porch. Adjacent to the property, over 1,200 acres of private land, to which guests have access, await exploration.

Getting There

Heading north from San Francisco, take Highway 101 to Ukiah, then Highway 253 (Boonville Road) west for 11 miles. From the coast, take Highway 128 to Boonville then Highway 253 east about six miles.

BENBOW INN

Address: 445 Lake Benbow Drive, Garberville, CA 95440
Telephone: (707) 923-2124
Hosts: Chuck and Patsy Watts
Room Rates: $68 to $210 double. Off season and holiday rates available
Credit Cards: American Express, Visa, MasterCard
Remarks: Complimentary afternoon-tea and scones; hot mulled wine in spring and fall; hors d'oeuvres daily. Closed after Thanksgiving until mid-April, except over Christmas holidays.

The throngs of Northern California's mighty redwoods part just enough to make room for a privileged few: the highway, Eel River, and the Benbow Inn.

The 1926 English Tudor inn rests on the banks of the Eel River and, in summer when the river is backed up, Lake Benbow. It is an elegant, historic hotel once frequented by the likes of Herbert Hoover, Eleanor Roosevelt and Charles Loughton. Through a succession of five owners, the inn underwent many changes and various states of disrepair. Present owners Chuck and Patsy Watts purchased the Benbow in 1978 after owning and operating a successful Carmel inn. In the years that followed, they restored the Benbow Inn to its former state of grace and grandeur, adding their own sensibilities and tastes. If the measure of a fine inn is its degree of comfort, then the Benbow ranks high.

Riverside Inn

The Benbow is edged by the gentle Eel River and a well-maintained lawn. All of the rooms in the four story inn offer a view of the river, the redwoods or the grounds. All 55 rooms have a private bath, air conditioning and central heating. Original art graces the walls, and a basket of amenities and another of books are a few of the extras. A carafe of sherry awaits arriving guests, and a coffee maker sits ready to perk. The Terrace and Garden rooms border the river and sport terraces with white lawn furniture. Three rooms feature a wood burning fireplace, VCR and refrigerator; one has a jacuzzi and wet bar.

Guests arriving in the afternoon may likely be swept from one form of merriment to another. Tea and scones are the mid-day ritual; hot mulled wine is offered in spring and fall. Both are served in the spacious lobby, decorated with antiques and jazz era relics. A plush burgundy couch, when not occupied by Truffles, the fudge-colored Afghan, is the spot to pursue a good novel or join others over a perplexing jigsaw puzzle. Glenn Miller music wafts from the juke box in the lounge, signaling it's time for hors d'oeuvres and a little cheer. The pub features a long mahagony bar and red leather love seats by the fire. A life-size stuffed bear sits casually at a window table, quietly sipping a martini and soaking in the atmosphere.

The comfortable outside patio is close to the Eel River.

Adjacent to the pub is a small theater where films are shown nightly. The Watts have a collection of over 250 classic films, which they will also show during the day upon request.

Fine Dining

The Benbow Inn restaurant resembles one you'd expect to find in the English countryside. It is a romantic spot for a leisurely meal, and the French chefs prepare the fresh California foods in innovative fashion. Breakfast, luncheon, Sunday brunch and dinner are available. Dinner reservations are recommended. The à la carte entrées, which vary seasonally, may include duck with lingonberries and apple, steak of lamb with rosemary, or poached salmon with bay scallops, red wine and fresh herbs. An extensive wine list offers an ample selection of fine wines to accompany the meal.

Sunday brunch features a selection of entrées including eggs Benbow, a seafood version of the popular eggs Benedict, which also appears on the menu. French doors lead to a terrace off the dining room, an enjoyable place from which to sample the fine cuisine and excellent service.

Special Events

Chuck and Patsy have created a calendar to list the many special events taking place at the inn. The Halloween Masquerade Ball is popular, as is the August Shakespeare in the Park. November is Wine Tasting, and December 31 is the annual Run for the Scones, in which guests run, walk or bike their way into the New Year. The inn is also an ideal spot for weddings or corporate gatherings.

Large outside windows allow plenty of refreshing sunlight in the rooms.

Plenty To Do

The Benbow Inn is located near a host of activities, so guests never lack something to do. With Lake Benbow at the doorstep, swimming, kayaking, windsurfing, and paddling are a must. The state park rents canoes and rowboats. There are hikes to take around the lake, and the park department has installed a self-guided exercise trail. A 9-hole golf course is nearby, as are several tennis courts. Horseback riding, bicycle rentals, and hayrides can be arranged by the front desk staff.

Visit the Giants

North of Garberville is a 33-mile scenic drive called the Avenue of the Giants. Following the South Fork of the Eel River, it winds through the Humboldt Redwoods State Park. Here, the tall redwoods are sometimes wide enough to drive through. In Scotia, a tidy community built entirely of redwood, is the Pacific Lumber Company mill. The largest redwood mill in the world, it offers an interesting visitor's center and self-guided tour.

Continuing north to Ferndale, visitors find a remarkable collection of Victorian homes. Picnic lunches are available for purchase from the dining room, and should be requested the night before.

Getting There

The inn is located 200 miles north of San Francisco and about 70 miles south of Eureka. Off Highway 1, take the Benbow Exit and head west on Lake Benbow Drive. The inn is just ahead on the left.

Heceta Head

Oregon

What Oregonians know, they're not saying. They're not letting on that their state is one of the last unspoiled regions of the country.

We found that Oregon is a state of small towns. Portland and Eugene are the only cities of any size, but the state is dotted with hundreds of small towns. If you search them out, you'll find old-time country stores dating from the 19th century, antique shops, historic homes and country inns, more than 50 covered bridges, small cheese and sausage factories, family vineyards, single-car ferries, craft shops and artists' studios.

Many of these small towns in western Oregon were once lumber towns. Mills employed just about everybody in town and logging trucks rumbled through the streets on their way to the mill. Much of that is gone now, moved elsewhere or gone out of business. In its place dozens of small tourism-related businesses are springing up, much to the delight of visitors.

A word about Oregonians. They are quite well aware that Oregon is one of the last unspoiled sections of the country. They strongly support environmental and preservation efforts and are fiercely opposed to commercial exploitation of their resources. The many Californians who have moved here in the last few years are among the staunchest defenders of Oregon the way it is.

That does not mean Oregonians are unfriendly or don't want visitors. On the contrary. Oregonians are among the friendliest and most welcoming folks you'll find anywhere. All they ask is that you have respect of their state the way they do.

Many pleasurable days can be spent meandering through the fertile valleys of Oregon's wine country, stopping at the various wineries for a sample. We'll often pick up a favorite wine, a loaf of fresh bread, a chunk of Tillamook cheese and a basket of ruby strawberries and settle under a shady tree for a couple of hours. That's Oregon's pace — one that flows at an easy tempo and often pauses for a couple of beats. In those pauses, we see what the Oregonians strive to preserve.

Natural Playground

Oregon is a state where people participate in the outdoors. The number of outdoor activities you can sample on a vacation is only limited by the amount of time you have to spend.

With 13 national forests, 11 wilderness areas, one national park, one national memorial, two national monuments, two recreational areas and more than 230 state parks, the opportunities are almost unlimited.

You can cast for salmon, steelhead and trout in more than 50,000 rivers, creeks and streams. Dozens of small ports strung along the Oregon coast offer charter fishing for salmon, tuna and bottom fish. River running has become a major sport in Oregon, and there are many rafting companies that will take you on a guided scenic or white water trip lasting a single day or several days. Wind surfing is very popular, particularly at Hood River at the eastern end of the Columbia Gorge. Many Oregon resort lakes offer boating, sailing and water skiing. If you'd rather let someone else do the driving, consider a trip up the Rogue on a jet boat or a trip on the Columbia aboard a sternwheeler.

Getting into the back country on horseback or on foot is easy. Ranches, resorts and stables offer everything from and afternoon's ride through the forest to extended pack trips into the Cascades. Hundreds of miles of trails, especially in the Cascades and Coast Range, beckon hikers and backpackers. You can hike from one end of Oregon to the other on the Pacific Crest Trail.

Oregon's coast is among the most captivating in the world. Miles of broad, quiet beaches prompt long walks in any season. Winter storms bring a bounty of driftwood and shells. Tidal pools thrive with delicate marine creatures. Charter fishing, windsurfing and kite flying are coastal pastimes.

The mighty Columbia River flows from its source in the Canadian Rockies to the Pacific Ocean in Astoria, forming the Washington-Oregon border. Just east of Portland, the river carves the magnificent Columbia Gorge, a wonderland of conservational, historical and recreational significance. The most spectacular view of the Gorge is obtained from the summit of 720-foot Crown Point. East of the summit, the impressive Multnomah Falls, one of the highest waterfalls in the nation, take a 620-foot plunge into the fast flowing Columbia.

The 11,235-foot Mt. Hood, just south of the Columbia Gorge, is abundantly forested and provides a healthy selection of outdoor activities for any season. Skiers enjoy the slopes which often stay open until well into summer.

Southern Oregon is home to a duet of mountains, the Cascades and Siskiyous. Two grand rivers, the Umpqua and Rogue, leave their source in the Cascades and continue to the Pacific Ocean. Just below the slopes of the mountains, clusters of sequined lakes gather, the largest being the Upper Klamath Lake.

Crater Lake is cradled at the crest of the Cascade Range. It rests in a deep caldera formed when the 12,000-foot volcano collapsed nearly 6,600 years ago. In winter, cross-country skiers traverse trails around the snow rimmed lake. In summer, it becomes a hiker's and photographer's paradise.

Central Oregon is the sun-saturated core of the state where over one hundred lakes and twice that many streams offer angling and rafting. The Deschutes River begins in the Cascades and pours down the eastern slopes, eventually joining the Columbia River. The Deschutes National Forest is dotted with sparkling alpine lakes and threaded with more than 100 miles of trails. Cross-country and Alpine skiers rejoice in the dry powder conditions found in this eastern region. After snow melt, equestrians find miles of quiet trails in the pine and sagebrush terrain.

Rock Hounding

Oregon is a treasure-trove of gemstones and fossils. Central Oregon offers recreational rock hounds the greatest concentration of areas for digging. Banded agate, crystal-lined geodes and jaspers are found near the Warm

Springs Indian Reservation. Thundereggs are found near Madras and Prineville, as are huge agate deposits. A commercial digging area northeast of Madras, off U.S. 97, maintains attended digging sites that yield blue agate, plume agate and green and red moss agate.

Oregon's Coast is the spot to look for jasper, petrified wood, Oregon jade (grossularite garnet) and agates. The cliffs near Tillamook, Newport, Coos Bay and Port Orford are prime fossil locations. Southern Oregon is known for its jaspers and milky chalcedony, as well as agates and geodes. Obsidian is found near Bend.

For information on geological field trips and rock hounding areas, contact:

Oregon Department of Geology and Mineral Industries
910 State Office Building
Portland, OR 97201
(503) 229-5580

Wineries

Over four dozen wineries straddle western Oregon's rolling hills. Long established as a fruit and berry growing region, the area is now covered with lush vineyards. Planted in the 1960s, the vines come from nobel European parentage. Different growing climates coupled with the distinctive skills of individual proprietors blend to create wines that are rapidly achieving international acclaim. Pinot Noirs, Rieslings, and Chardonnays are among the award-winning wines produced in Oregon. In Washington County, within a 35-mile radius of Portland, there are seven primary wineries. Yamhill County, within a 20-mile radius of Portland, hosts 19 wineries. Southern Oregon's Umpqua Valley, near Roseburg, has six new wineries. Another two dozen are found throughout the inland and coastal regions.

Most Oregon wineries open their doors to the public, offering tours and tasting rooms. Hours vary, so it is best to check ahead. A brochure with local maps and winery listings is available by writing to:

Oregon Winegrowers Association
1324 S.W. 21st Avenue
Portland, OR 97201

Liquor Laws

Liquor is sold by the bottle in state liquor stores and by the glass in restaurants and lounges. Wine and beer are sold at grocery stores. The legal age for alcohol consumption is 21 years. Also note: The Oregon State Patrol and local police use radar.

Weather

The Cascade mountain range is the predominate factor in determining Oregon's weather patterns. Pacific Ocean marine air creates a generally mild environment west of the Cascades; east of the mountains the climate is drier, creating greater temperature variations.

Information Sources For Oregon

Oregon maintains staffed travel information centers at key border points around the state from April through October. These centers provide extensive information to visitors. Unstaffed Travel Info Centers are located along Oregon's main highway arteries (I-5, I-84, U.S. 101, U.S. 97). Gazebos display pictorial and written information on scenic and recreational attractions. Other useful information sources are as follows:

Oregon Economic Development Department
Tourism Division
595 Cottage Street N.E.
Salem, Oregon 97310
(800) 547-7842 (outside Oregon)
(800) 233-3306 (within Oregon)

State Parks and Recreation Division
525 Trade Street S.E.
Salem, OR 97310
(503) 378-6305

Oregon Department of Fish and Wildlife
P.O. Box 3503
Portland, OR 97208

U.S. Forest Service
319 S.W. Pine Street
P.O. Box 3623
Portland, OR 97208
(503) 221-2877

U.S. Fish and Wildlife Service
500 N.E. Multnomah
Portland, OR 97232
(503) 231-6828

Oregon Coast Association
P.O. Box 670
Newport, OR 97365
(503) 336-5107

Greater Portland Convention and Visitors Association
26 Southwest Salmon Street
Portland, OR 97204
(503) 222-2223

Selected Oregon Events

January
"World's Toughest Rodeo" — Portland
Great Northwest Chili Cookoff — Portland

February
Oregon Shakespearean Festival Begins — Ashland
Newport Seafood and Wine Festival — South Beach

March
Beachcomber Festival — Brookings
Blessing of the Fleet — Garibaldi

April
Great Crab Feed and Seafood Festival — Astoria
Blossom Festival — Hood River
Rowing Regatta — Riverplace in Portland

May
All Northwest Ballad Contest and Gay 90's Festival — Forest Grove
Spring Kite Festival — Lincoln City
Maritime Week — Astoria

June
Rose Festival Parade and Starlight Run — Portland
Fort Vancouver Days — Vancouver (WA)

July
Peter Britt Music Festival — Jacksonville
Columbia Gorge Pro-Am Speed Slalom — Hood River

August
Mt. Hood Festival of Jazz — Mt. Hood
Antique Air Show — Vancouver (WA)
Columbia Gorge Blowout — Hood River

September
Oregon State Fair — Salem
Annual Vancouver Sausage Festival — Vancouver (WA)
Annual "Autumn Fest" — Portland

October
Harvest Festival — Hood River
Llama Show — Grants Pass

November
Verboort Kraut and Sausage Festival — Hood River
Annual Harvest Festival — Portland

December
Twelve Days of Christmas — Ashland
Handel Festival — Portland

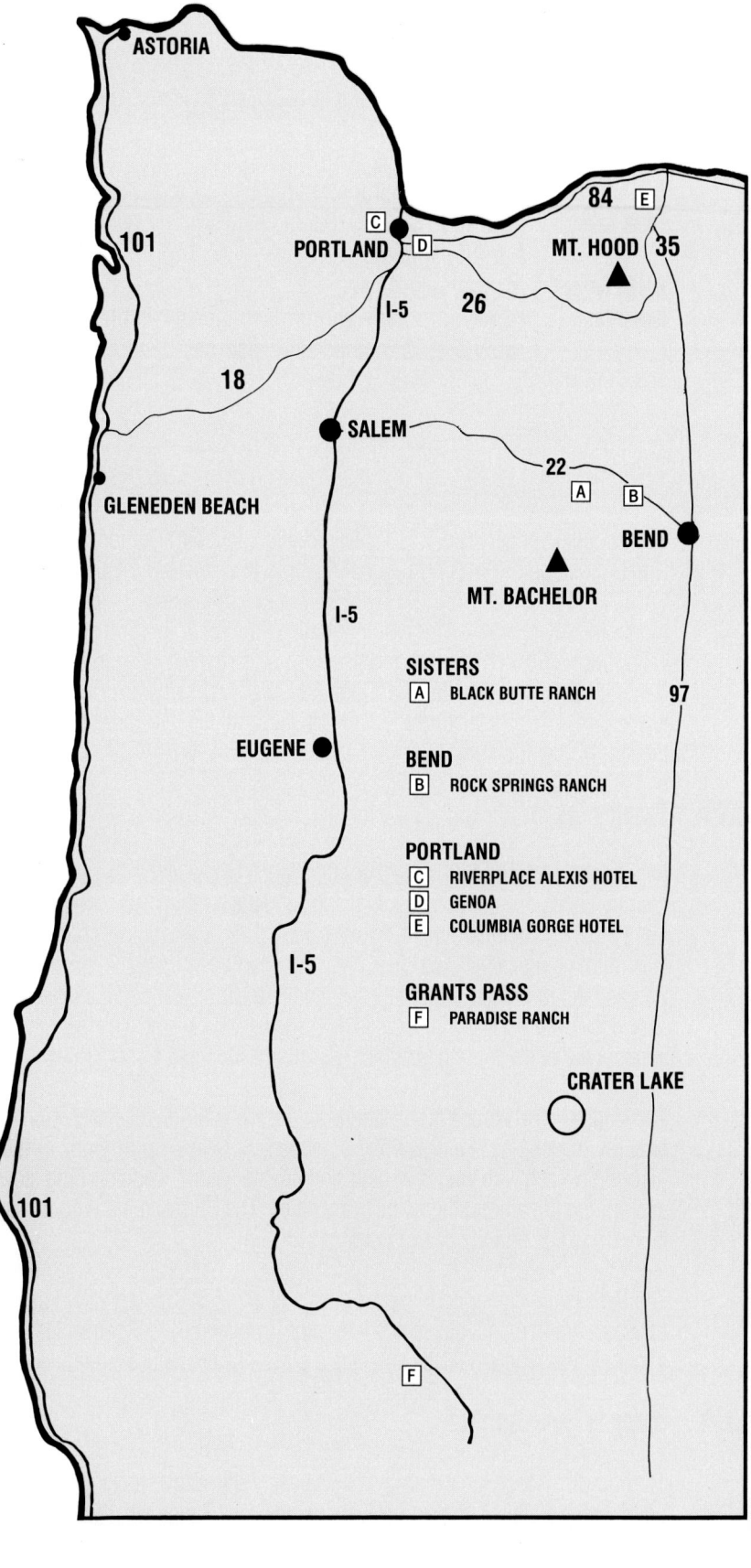

ASTORIA

101

PORTLAND ⬚C
⬚D

84 ⬚E

MT. HOOD 35

I-5

26

18

SALEM

22

⬚A ⬚B

BEND

GLENEDEN BEACH

I-5

▲
MT. BACHELOR

SISTERS
⬚A   BLACK BUTTE RANCH

97

EUGENE ●

BEND
⬚B   ROCK SPRINGS RANCH

PORTLAND
⬚C   RIVERPLACE ALEXIS HOTEL
⬚D   GENOA
⬚E   COLUMBIA GORGE HOTEL

I-5

GRANTS PASS
⬚F   PARADISE RANCH

CRATER LAKE

○

101

⬚F

PARADISE RANCH INN

Address: 7000-D Monument Drive, Grants Pass, OR 97526
Telephone: (503) 479-4333
Hosts: Mattie and Ollie Raymond,
Resident General Managers
Room Rates: $69.50 to $96.50 single, $79.50 to $99.50 double.
Additional person $20.
Credit Cards: MasterCard, Visa
Remarks: Honeymoon and winter packages available at special
rates. Pets and children welcome.

The Rogue River carves a broad valley through southern Oregon, pausing in Grants Pass before making its final 50-mile journey to the Pacific Ocean. Sheltered by the coast and Siskiyou Mountains, the valley is graced with a moderate, dry climate year-round. Paradise Ranch Inn, on 300 acres in the valley floor, provides an excellent base from which to enjoy this scenic region. General managers Mattie and Ollie Raymond operate the inn with the assistance of family members. "We want guests to feel like they are a part of the family, like the ranch belongs to them," says Mattie.

Country Estate

Rimmed by a bright white fence, Paradise Ranch Inn resembles a gentleman's country estate. It was, in fact, a homestead cattle ranch when it was built in 1913. A white clapboard ranch house contains 18 guest rooms, six of which face onto a man-made pond. Country American decor prevails throughout. Rooms are furnished with queen- and king-size beds, and a spacious bathroom features a double-headed tiled shower. In keeping with the tranquil atmosphere of the inn, no televisions or phones are in the rooms.

The House in the Woods is set apart from the inn, offering total seclusion for families or couples. Fully kitchen equipped, it sleeps up to eight in four bedrooms, each with king-size beds and private bath. A wood burning stove and hot tub are among the home's amenities. The House in the Woods may be rented in its entirety or by the room.

The Barn is the gathering place for guests of all ages. The recreation center houses a grand piano, big screen television, pool and Ping-Pong tables, and a lounge area where guests can enjoy a glass of wine before dinner.

Dining in Paradise

The Paradise Ranch Inn's dining room is beautifully set overlooking a tranquil pond. In the distance, the many layers of the Coast Range are highlighted by gentle mist and the setting sun. The dining room is presided over by one of

The restaurant overlooks ponds and the golfing area.

Southern Oregon's finest chefs, who produces excellent cuisine based on seasonally available foods. Home grown vegetables and herbs are used, as well as only the freshest local meats and seafoods. Rack of lamb, scampi New Orleans, and Châteaubriand for Two are favorite dinner entrées. Chocolate-orange decaffinated coffee is the perfect accompaniment to the tempting array of desserts. A Hearty Ranch Breakfast and the Paradise Continental Breakfast get the day off to a fine start, and include homemade goods. Box lunches are available by request. A complete wine list features selections from Oregon as well as several imports.

Sense of Belonging

"What makes Paradise Ranch Inn special is that guests have a sense of belonging," says Mattie. "We have guests coming with their kids who came here as kids themselves."

Two lighted tennis courts on the grounds are utilized by guests for a nominal court fee. A tennis professional is available for private and group lessons as well as a stroke analysis video session. A ball machine may be rented on an hourly basis.

The swimming pool is the place to cool off after a game of tennis, and the hot tub swirls away those aches and pains. The ponds are stocked with trout and large mouth bass, and paddle boats are ready on the shore for an evening spin. A small island in the pond is equipped with a barbeque and a gazebo. It is an ideal spot for weddings and other special occasions. The inn has a fleet of mountain bikes available for guests' use, and maintains a couple of miles of trails for walking or riding. A three-hole triangular pitch-and-putt course provides family fun.

All the events of the Rogue River Valley are nearby.

The latest addition to Paradise Ranch Inn is an 18-hole golf course, targeted for completion in late 1988. With the completion of the course, additional guest rooms will be built.

Diverse Offerings

The Rogue River Valley offers a diversity of attractions, not the least of which is the Rogue River itself. Grants Pass is the headquarters for several licensed guides who offer fishing excursions on the river. One- to four-day trips are available on kayaks, rafts, drift boats and paddle boats. A two-hour jet boat departs Grants Pass for 250-foot deep Hellgate Canyon. For landlubbers, a paved road winds along the Rogue northwest of Grants Pass, and hiking trails weave into the wild river section where no cars are allowed. The Rogue, where sturgeon, steelhead and salmon are at their peak during winter, spring and fall, is a year-round playground.

The charming town of Ashland, nestled in the green foothills of the Siskiyous, is just south of Grants Pass along Interstate 5. Ashland is known for its excellent Shakespearean theater, the festival which lasts from late February through October. Jacksonville, just 20 minutes from Ashland, conducts the Britt classical, bluegrass, jazz, dance and musical theater festivals from late June through September 1 in the beautiful Peter Britt gardens.

Getting There

From southbound I-5, take the Hugo Exit and turn right onto Monument Drive. Proceed 3.9 miles to the Paradise Ranch Inn, on your right. From northbound I-5, proceed to the Merlin Exit, north of Grants Pass. Turn right onto Monument Drive. The inn is 1.9 miles down the road on the left.

BLACK BUTTE RANCH LODGE & RESORT

Address:	P.O. Box 8000, Black Butte Ranch, OR 97759
Telephone:	(503) 595-6211, reservations (800) 452-7455 in OR
Location:	On U.S. Highway 20, eight miles west of Sisters
Host:	Mike Gallagher, Vice President and General Manager
Room Rates:	$45 standard room, $60 deluxe room, $90 to $140 one- to three-bedroom condo apartments, $80 to $150 two- to four-bedroom homes. Minimum stays during the summer season.
Credit Cards:	American Express, Discover, MasterCard, Visa
Remarks:	No pets, no fireworks, no motorcycles, scooters or off-road vehicles.

On the eastern slopes of Oregon's Cascade range, the ponderosa pine grow tall and stately, providing valuable habitat for deer, coyote, porcupine and raccoon. Eagles and osprey build their nests high in the pine's boughs, and squirrels, chipmunks and quail gather their seeds for food. At the 3,300-foot level, the pine give way to meadows and lakes, and it is here that Black Butte Ranch, Oregon's great golf and tennis resort, lies. Surrounded by seven Cascade peaks that range from the 6,415-foot cinder cone called Black Butte to the proud 10,495-foot Mount Jefferson, you might think that Black Butte Ranch would be dwarfed by comparison. Not at all. Sitting on the patios and decks of the ranch's condos and homes to watch the sun first light on the meadow, you would be hard-pressed to tell where the ranch ends and the Cascades begin.

Not a Carbon Copy

Black Butte Ranch is a destination resort unlike any other. Each unit in the 1,830-acre development is individually furnished and privately owned, but many are managed by the reservation desk. The units have fully stocked kitchens (often including a dishwasher), washer, dryer, a rock or brick fireplace, television and telephone, wide inviting deck, daily housekeeping, and, most importantly, room to breathe. Guests receive the same privileges accorded the owners: full access to two golf courses, four swimming pools, 19 tennis courts, miles and miles of bike and jogging paths, and the lodge.

The lodge is the one building owned and operated by Black Butte Ranch. The three-story glass, fir and pine building is made all the more grand by the scale of the scenery outside its floor-to-ceiling windows. The furnishings combine antique tables and secretaries with modern oak and fabric chairs. Accent rugs and tall potted plants cover the wooden floors. The rental accommodation desk and property sales office comprise the first level; the second houses the Lt. Henry Abbot and Elijah Sparks conference rooms, the restaurant and kitchen. On the uppermost floor, with an unrivaled view of the Cascades, is the lounge, where you can enjoy a full-service bar and nightly entertainment.

The main lodge with meeting rooms, restaurant and lounge.

Conference facilities and a highly qualified staff who understand the importance of your meetings are available for small groups at the Lodge.

Ranchmade Specialties

The restaurant, with its ringside seats overlooking Big Meadow and the 350 head of cattle that graze there, is renowned in central Oregon for its fine seafood and steaks. But the chefs don't stop there. Ranch dinner specialties include generous cuts of prime rib, casserole of sole (baked with crabmeat, wine sauce and chccsc), breast of Oregon chicken, roast duck with orange sauce, sautéed chicken breast meunière and wiener schnitzel. The wine list contains 90 red, white and sparkling vintages from Oregon, California, Washington and France.

Breakfast specialties include giant cinnamon rolls, ranchmade granola, eggs Benedict, hot scones, and an omelette brimming with fresh ingredients. Lunch is an assortment of deli sandwiches, salads, a hot kettle of soup and fresh ranchmade bread, cheeses and fruit.

The Sporting Life

Golf is the main recreational activity at Black Butte Ranch. Residents and guests play on two immaculately groomed 18-hole courses located amid the trees and within view of the mountains and lakes. Both the Big Meadow and Glaze Meadow courses are par 72 and are open seven days a week. The facilities include a driving range, practice greens and a pro shop. The ranch offers golf clinics throughout the summer, and golf pros are available to assist you with your game.

The resort has two 18-hole par 72 courses.

If golf has a rival at the ranch, that rival's name is tennis. There are 19 Plexi-Pave courts in seven different locations. In addition to special instruction classes for teens and adults, guests can arrange for private or semiprivate lessons. The ranch's sport shops rent rackets and ball machines.

Swimmers have no problem cooling off on Oregon's hot, dry summer days, for the ranch has four large pools and several wading pools for the little ones. Other activities include canoeing, or nearby horseback riding and whitewater rafting. There is fishing on the Deschutes and Metolius rivers or on Lodge Lake. The ranch also offers 18 miles of paved biking trails.

In the winter, the Lodge Sport Shop rents cross-country skis. The Lodge offers rooms with discounted downhill ski packages at nearby Hoodoo Ski Bowl.

Sisters, the small Western town eight miles east of the ranch, has only three streets, yet more than 70 businesses, shops and restaurants line them. Known as the llama capital of North America, the community has become a center for llama ranches. Should you choose not to leave the grounds, you can drive to the ranch's store for an amazing variety of foodstuff. The two sport shops sell books and magazines, clothing, and sporting equipment.

Getting There

U.S. Highway 97 is the main route through central Oregon. From the north, drive to Redmond, then turn onto Highway 126 and head for Sisters. From the south, drive to Bend, then take Highway 20 to Sisters. From the west, take Highway 22 from Salem, or Highway 126 from Eugene, which merges with Highway 20. The well-marked ranch turnoff is eight miles west of town.

ROCK SPRINGS RANCH

Address: 64201 Tyler Road, Bend, OR 97701
Telephone: (503) 382-1957
Locations: Nine miles north of Bend
Host: John Gill, General Manager
Room Rates: $745 single, $1,350 double, per week, late June
through Labor Day, American Plan; family rates are
lower. Holiday rates from $68 per person, per day,
modified American Plan.
Credit Cards: MasterCard, Visa, Diners Club
Remarks: No pets.

Nestled in the ponderosa pine and juniper tree country of central Oregon's Cascade foothills is Rock Springs Ranch, a comfortable, unpretentious place where guests quickly get to know each other and become part of an extended family. It is a place with strong traditions and ties. In fact, over half of the guests return each year. At Rock Springs, guests usually gather in the lodge after dinner to play cards or chess, or just sit in front of the fire and chat.

Donna Gill, a lean, sinewy septuagenarian who was as comfortable splitting wood as she was riding a horse, is another tradition at the ranch — she's even a bit of a legend in this part of Oregon. Donna ran the ranch until she passed away less than a decade ago. She built the ranch with families in mind. Her nephew John now operates Rock Springs and continues the family tradition.

Catering to Families

Rock Springs caters to families. Youngsters have their own counselors and programs to involve them in horseback riding, evening hayrides and lunch rides, organized talent shows, hikes, swimming and craft projects. And, while children are off exploring, adults have a chance to spend a little time together or join others at the cocktail hour. Families with children under five who require one-to-one supervision are invited to bring along their own babysitter. The ranch will provide sleeping accommodations and meals free of charge.

Eleven cozy, modern cabins are scattered among the tall ponderosa pines. Some have cathedral ceilings and knotty pine walls and accommodate six. Most have a fireplace; wood is stacked outside the door. Some cabins also have a kitchen, so you can prepare a snack or a full meal for yourself whenever you're hungry.

Rock Springs Ranch operates on an American Plan from the end of June until early September. The week's package, which runs from Saturday to Saturday, includes all meals and activities. When winter comes, a modified American plan, which includes breakfast and dinner, is offered.

Some of the rooms sleep up to six people.

Nature's Song

In the early morning you wake to the songs of meadowlarks. The breeze through the trees sounds like distant surf. You're apt to see big gray, bushy-tailed squirrels, or bald and golden eagles that come to fish in the pond.

John Gill keeps about 55 horses for his guests, and great care and attention is paid to the fitness of the riding stock. Whether a guest is a beginner in need of instructions or an eager, advanced rider, he or she can really enjoy the challenge and excitement of riding at Rock Springs. Once riders are assigned their horses, they are divided into small groups according to ability and set off on trails through the adjoining Deschutes National Forest, which is set against the backdrop of the magnificent snow-covered peaks of the Three Sisters.

For those who prefer not to ride, there is a swimming pool, lighted tennis courts, volleyball, horseshoes, croquet, fishing in the pond (stocked with bass and trout) and the option of doing nothing at all. The ranch also makes a good base for day trips to attractions in the Bend area. Among the favorites are Oregon High Desert Museum, Mount Bachelor for skiing (into July), Tumalo Falls, Pilot Butte State Park, fly fishing in top-rated Deschutes River, the spectacular scenery of Cove Palisades State Park, a day with the Indians on the Warm Springs Reservation and Lava Lands Visitors Center, Newberry Crater and the volcanic country south of Bend. There are also seven golf courses nearby.

At the end of the day, when activity slows and muscles grow tired, relax in the ranch's custom outdoor spa. Warm water spews from jets in the tiled bath set into a relaxing cave-like shelter of boulders.

Ride through interesting terrain.

Well-Fed Guests

Rock Springs Ranch feeds its guests well. Meals are served family style from the buffet. Breakfasts may include omelettes, homemade sticky buns, French toast, pancakes, waffles, fresh fruit and juices, ham, sausage or bacon and eggs. For lunch you can expect one hot dish plus sandwiches, soup, salad and cookies. Dinner ranges from seafood or Mexican cuisine to turkey or prime rib with a choice of two entrées, vegetables, salad, fresh-baked bread and dessert. The main meal often centers around a particular theme ranging from Hawaiian to Cajun to Western barbeque.

Between meals, guests can nibble from a bowl of fresh fruit or a plate of cookies that are always kept well stocked. The ranch also provides plenty of lemonade, iced tea, coffee, and assorted hot teas to quench your thirst.

A Refreshing Environment for Gatherings

During the fall, winter and spring, the ranch turns its efforts toward government and corporate meetings. Rock Springs provides the meeting rooms, the equipment and the food service to ensure a refreshing environment for productive meetings. Distractions are few during the off-season, and the ranch handles only one group at a time. Weddings and private receptions may be arranged, as well as custom ski packages for groups numbering 20 to 50.

Getting There

To reach Rock Springs, follow U.S. 20 north from Bend for six miles to Tumalo. Turn west on the Tumalo Reservoir Road and follow signs for three miles to the ranch.

RIVERPLACE ALEXIS HOTEL

Address: 1510 Southwest Harbor Way, Portland, OR 97201
Telephone: (503) 228-3233
Location: On the Willamette River in downtown Portland
Host: Celinda Carlisle Knott, General Manager
Room Rate: $135 to $140 double, $140 to $500 suites. Weekend rates available.
Credit Cards: American Express, Carte Blanche, Diners Club, MasterCard, Visa
Remarks: Continental breakfast included in room rates.

"The RiverPlace Alexis Hotel is a resort in the middle of a city," says general manager Celinda Carlisle Knott. "We offer all the amenities of a big resort, yet we are a small luxury hotel."

The RiverPlace Alexis borders Portland's new riverside esplanade. The clapboard and brick structure combines the pastel elegance of a New England farmhouse with the cozy look of an Amsterdam rowhouse. Lovely window boxes and lively windsocks add a festive flair. The front yard is the Willamette River and a yacht basin which is haven to sailboats, powerboats, and racks of rowing shells. Condos rise above a row of neighboring shops and restaurants —a designer deli, a bookstore "for the soul," and a neighborhood concierge. It is a compact European village with distinct Northwest overtones.

First-Rate Service

The RiverPlace Alexis, which opened in 1985, uniquely fills the needs of the savvy business traveler as well as the discriminating pleasure traveler. It offers the warmth one would expect of a bed and breakfast, yet the sophistication of a fine hotel. Of its 74 guest rooms, 24 are suites. All rooms are spacious and airy and decorated in a specially created palette of colors that brighten even the gloomiest of Northwest days. Periwinkle accents on a pale yellow theme lend a light touch. Thick carpeting, handcrafted rugs, and botanical prints add a homey warmth. Six of the rooms feature a wood burning fireplace. A handmade tile wet bar, refrigerator and whirlpool bath grace others. Many rooms offer a view of the marina.

"What it all comes down to is service," Celinda says. "Our staff sees guests as real people." From the moment you arrive, when a smiling valet greets you at your car, to check-out time when the bellman calls you by name, the modus operandi is full-on service. Few other hotels would think to review the guest list in order to have home country flags flying upon the foreign traveler's arrival. Complimentary sherry, cozy terry robes, fresh flowers in all public areas, twice daily maid service with nightly turndown, a multilingual staff, and morning newspaper delivered to the door are but a few of the attentive

Dine overlooking the Willamette River.

gestures. A trip to the private sauna and spa begins with the bellman escort from your room. A Continental breakfast (included in the room rate) may be enjoyed in the hotel's Esplanade Restaurant or in your room. Twenty-four hour room service and limosine service are among the finishing touches.

Eight condo units adjacent to the hotel are available for long term rental (one week at least). All feature river views, washer and dryer, and a complete kitchen, a convenient addition for those longer stays.

The hotel is ideally suited to the needs of the professional. Banquet and meeting rooms accommodate up to 200 for dining and 400 for receptions. while more intimate rooms are designed for smaller groups.

Riverside Dining

The Alexis offers a trio of dining spots: the Esplanade Restaurant, The Patio, and The Bar. The Esplanade, serving breakfast, lunch, and dinner, seats 83 in the bi-level dining room overlooking the marina. Fresh Northwest cuisine is highlighted with a selection of seafoods, poultry and meats. Ragout of prawns and scallops, Dungeness crab with tamari, ginger and scallions, and filet of beef with wild mushrooms and brandy, are but a few of the innovative entrées.

The Patio serves light patio fare (mesquite-grilled burgers, gourmet sausages, salads) in the summer months. Lunches range from the best burger in town to clams and mussels in white wine and herbs. You can enjoy live entertainment five times a week here while contemplating the panoramic view of the river. The nightly Cognac Hour (two for the price of one), and sumptuous dessert bar can turn into an indulent all-you-can-eat feast.

The Grand Suite is ideal for entertaining.

A Walking Tour

One of the best ways to see Portland is to merely step out the front door of the RiverPlace Alexis and begin walking. Adjacent to the hotel is Tom McCall Park, a wide green lawn that parallels the Willamette. Jogging trails wind along the riverbank through the park. The nearby Portland Art Museum houses 35 centuries of world art in its extensive collections acquired over the past 90 years. Northwest Coast Indian Art, Asian, West African, American and European art are all exhibited.

Portland's most historic buildings are found in the Skidmore/Old Town Historical District, the largest remaining concentration of 19th century cast iron west of the Mississippi. Cafes, specialty shops and a marketplace add to the area's charm.

Yamhill Marketplace, in the Yamhill Historic District, is a five-level glass atrium containing more than 50 shops. Just north of the Yamhill District is Chinatown. Oriental imports, old and new artifacts, ethnic grocery stores and restaurants are found in these colorful blocks. The Riverplace Alexis' location makes it ideal for strolling the Esplanade shops or watching the activity on the busy waterfront. A nearby company rents small rowboats for a trip on the Willamette River.

Getting There

To reach the RiverPlace Alexis, follow signs to City Center-Front Street. Take Front Avenue to Market Street. Head south on Market Street following signs to RiverPlace Marina. Stay in the far left lane. Turn left at the first traffic signal onto Montgomery Street. Turn left on Harbor Way. The hotel is at the end of Harbor Way.

GENOA

Address:	2832 Southeast Belmont Street, Portland, OR 97214
Telephone:	(503) 238-1464
Hosts:	Amelia and Fred Hard
Cuisine:	Northern Italian
Prices:	Seven-course dinner, $32; four-course dinner, $24
Credit Cards:	American Express, Carte Blanche, Diners Club, MasterCard, Visa
Hours:	Seven-course dinner seatings from 6 to 9:30 p.m. on the hour and half-hour, four-course dinner seatings only at 5:30, 6, 10, and 10:30 p.m. Monday through Saturday.

Portland's modest eastside holds a surprising dining find. Genoa, a fine Italian restaurant, hides under an inconspicuous canopy in an unlikely neighborhood. The one-room bistro, painted in deep muted browns, exudes a quietly understated elegance when shadows from the table candles dance playfully on the walls. Italian caneback chairs, select antiques, and a decorative Oriental rug accent the unpretentious decor. Best of all, Genoa's cuisine reflects the same refinement and sensibility.

Prix Fixe

Genoa is known for its seven-course, fixed price dinner. The approximately two- to three-hour meal takes you on a leisurely tour of Northern Italian cuisine. The three senior cooks rotate duties semi-monthly; each is responsible for researching, designing, testing, and preparing their feasts for a two-week period. The result: a fresh, innovative meal and a constantly new dining experience.

Just as each cook takes pride in the meal design, the servers take pride in the presentation. The deliberate lack of hierarchy in the restaurant management creates an atmosphere of cooperation in which each employee works with a sense of individual responsibility. Present owners Amelia and Fred Hard were also employees of the restaurant before purchasing it. "We were determined to keep it nurtured and growing," says Amelia.

Northern Italian Extravaganza

Genoa has achieved high ratings from restaurant reviewers. *Oregon Magazine* ranked it one of the 10 best restaurants in the state. The secret: fine, fresh foods and delightful, delicate seasonings.

The meal begins with antipasto, which in summer might be proscuitto and melon or lime-marinated salmon. The winter antipasto is bagna cauda, a hot fondue of cream, anchovy and garlic served with crisp vegetables and homemade sourdough breadsticks for dipping. An innovative soup follows, perhaps yellow zucchini in chicken broth with marsala and garlic accents, or cream of carrot. Homemade pasta, which is always fresh, comes next. A fish course follows, perhaps red snapper with a light white wine and lemon sauce, topped with cinnamon, pine nuts and orange slices, or oysters baked with crème fraiche, mushrooms, bread crumbs and fresh marjoram.

Of seven courses, the only choices to be made are in the entrées and the desserts. Three entrées are offered, including seafood, fowl and meat. Scallops sautéed with capers, shallots and red peppers, veal in a sage cream sauce, or roasted quail with stuffing are just a few entrée possibilities.

Genoa's dazzling dessert tray features over 100 recipes. Layered tortes, fruit tarts, creamy gelato and rich chocolate dessert are among the possibilities. Coffee, espresso, cappuccino and dessert wines are offered to round out the meal, followed by a selection of fresh fruits.

A lengthy wine list offers Italian, French, California and Northwest wines sure to please most palates and purses. Aperitifs may be ordered before the meal.

Genoa is a favorite with Portland theater-goers who enjoy a four-course version of the full spread before or after the show. Reservations are strongly advised on weekdays, and are required on weekends.

Getting There

From downtown Portland, go east over the Morrison Street Bridge. The street becomes Belmont. Continue approximately one and one-half miles.

Experience why *Bon Appétit* calls Genoa "uncommonly sophisticated."

COLUMBIA GORGE HOTEL

Address: 4000 West Cliff Drive, Hood River, OR 97031
Telephone: (503) 386-5566, (800) 345-1921
Location: On the western outskirts of Hood River, 61 miles east of Portland
Hosts: Geoff Moore and Seaberg Einarsson, Directing Managers
Room Rates: $95 to $175, double
Credit Cards: American Express, Diners Club, MasterCard, Visa, Discover
Remarks: Rates include ''World Famous Farm Breakfast''

The mighty Columbia River surges at its feet. Majestic Mt. Hood protrudes at its back. Phelps Creek, which takes a final dramatic 203-foot leap to join the powerful river below, meanders through its 13 acres of flowered grounds. The Columbia Gorge Hotel has a most spectacular setting indeed.

This elegant inn is as rich with history as it is beauty. Oregon lumber magnate Simon Benson, prime mover behind the Columbia River Gorge Scenic Highway project and builder of Portland's Benson Hotel, saw the potential. In 1921, he opened the Columbia Gorge Hotel, a 42-room, three story inn boasting "all with bath" and the state's only ballroom east of Portland.

Soon, the magic was felt and the hotel's reputation grew. In the midst of the Jazz Age, the Columbia Gorge Hotel became a favorite retreat for the "idle rich." Famous guests, such as Rudolph Valentino and Clara Bow, were said to have stayed here, and some even had rooms named after them.

The hotel changed hands several times over the years, and eventually became victim of the nation's economic climate. In 1952 it became a retirement home, and suffered sorely from neglect. 1978 brought new owners, the hotel was restored, and its renewed grandeur re-earned it the title "Waldorf of the West."

All That Jazz

The hotel's exterior, with red tile roof, mustard yellow stucco walls and shuttered windows, is somewhat reminiscent of a Spanish monastery. Entering the foyer, however, the feeling of the Flapper Era begins to take hold. Massive plastered beams, a glittery chandelier, swinging French doors and glass doorknobs take you back 60 years. Just off the lobby is the Valentino Lounge, a plush gathering place for sipping cocktails and enjoying music.

All 42 rooms are different. Antique furniture and authentic replicas (gooseneck rockers, overstuffed chairs) create an warm uncluttered look. A few rooms offer a fireplace, another features a wood canopy bed. Rooms 239 and 339 are directly above the Wah-Gwin-Gwin Falls.

The restaurant provides wonderful views down into the gorge.

The hotel has become a respected host to corporate and private groups: the Benson Ballroom, with its removable dance floor, is ideal for meetings, banquets and weddings; the Falls Room is well suited for smaller groups.

Famous Food

The Columbia Gorge Hotel prides itself on its trademarked "World Famous Farm Breakfast" which, by all counts, is enough food to provide sustenance for a week. Upward of 17 varieties of fruits are displayed on individual dishes. Next, a steaming baked apple arrives, followed closely by a crock of oatmeal. Three eggs, ham, sausage links, bacon and hash browns are served with country biscuits and the famed "honey from the sky." Save room for the stack of hotcakes that complete the meal because, like the menu says, it's not a choice — you get it all. Coffee, tea and chilled champagne are all available.

The dining room overlooks the river. At night, in the soft candlelight, it becomes a romantic spot for enjoying a leisurely meal and watching the lights on the opposite shore. The excellent service is accentuated by tableside flambés and sautés. The varied menu includes Oregon favorites such as Columbia River sturgeon and rack of eastern Oregon lamb which Chef David Craignic prepares in a creative fashion. Peppercorn filet medallions and Columbia River salmon round out the entrée offerings. The wine list, with over 600 offerings, highlights wines from the Pacific Northwest, in addition to a wide selection of California and French vintages.

Gorge Yourself

The hotel is a wonderful base for the many activities found in this region. The Gorge has become a mecca for windsurfers in the last few years — westerly

Manicured grounds surround the hotel.

winds blow up to 60 miles per hour and an opposing current flows up to six knots, creating ideal conditions for skilled board sailors. From the hotel and other vantage points, you can watch the vibrantly colored sails jumping and jibing through the waves. Bonneville Lock and Dam, the first hydroelectric powerhouse in the area, offers a visitor's center along the Washington shore of the Columbia. Watch grain barges navigate the locks and, from April to October, see salmon climb fish ladders on their upstream journey. For a closer look at the river, the 145-foot sternwheeler *Columbia Gorge*, an authentic replica of an 1800s paddlewheeler, departs and returns to Cascade Locks three times each day.

High adventure is found in fishing for Columbia Gorge sturgeon that can reach lengths of 15 feet in their century-long lifespan. Whitewater rafting, horseback riding, and hiking are other activities in the area. The hotel will gladly arrange these for guests.

In spring, white apple blossoms blanket the slopes. By fall, rich harvests are en route to packing sheds. Try driving the Mount Hood loop, Oregon 35, and climb through orchards to supreme vantage points of the Columbia River below. Cross 4,157-foot Barlow Pass along one of the routes used by Oregon Trail pioneers in the 1840s. In spring, wild pink rhododendrens abound, in fall, a profusion of vibrant autumn colors splash the hillside.

Getting There

Take Interstate 84 east from Portland and turn off at Exit 62. Cross the highway and turn left on West Cliff Drive. The hotel is ahead on your right. Amtrak offers service from Portland on the *Pioneer*, and the hotel will arrange transportation from Hood River station.

Friday Harbor

Washington

Washington State is the strong shoulder of a broad nation. The face of the land displays a rugged beauty; its natives reveal a sinewy character, wrought from the robust mettle of their pioneer ancestry. Washington is a masterwork of intense, natural grandeur and genuine, hearty people.

Two impressive mountain ranges, the Cascades and the Olympics, run north-south ribbons through the state. Broken by crags, bluffs and deep canyons, the Cascade range extends some 750 miles from British Columbia into northern California. Washington's Mount Rainier, reaching a height of 14,410 feet, is the highest peak in the Cascades. Its neighbor to the south, Mt. Saint Helens, achieved international recognition after its major eruption in May, 1980. The mountains are flanked with dense evergreens and accented by vibrant meadows and mountain flowers. Alpine lakes hide in glacial valleys; countless streams plummet down steep cliffs.

Four highways cross the Cascade range, descending into Eastern Washington. This southeast corner of the state is the cradle of Washington's history: Lewis and Clark followed a centuries-old trail into what is now the heart of Walla Walla. Eastern Washington's expansive plateau is one of the world's most productive wheat growing regions. When the drizzle of the Cascades falls on Western Washington, natives flock eastward to this region's 4,000 lakes and miles of rivers.

West of the Cascade Range is Puget Sound and the state's largest city, Seattle. This sparkling "Emerald City" is 80 percent surrounded by water. Seattle continually ranks high marks on polls of "most liveable cities." The city proudly retains a sense of its past, when it thrived as a gold rush town.

Seattle is edged by Puget Sound, Washington's protected inland waterway stretching 90 miles from its southern tip to the Strait of Juan de Fuca. This passageway bustles with freighters, tugs, pleasure craft and state ferries. The 172 islands of the San Juan archipelago, linked by small inlets and intricate passes, are scattered like stepping stones to Canada. Many islands are inhabited year-round, others are a floating playground. The "banana belt" climate, combined with a bounty of fresh seafoods, attracts sailors, fishermen, kayakers and scuba divers, motorists and bicyclists.

National Parks

Washington State contains three national parks: Mount Rainier, Olympic, and North Cascade. Mt. Rainier, locally referred to as "The Mountain," looms awesomely at the western edge of the Cascade Range. A dormant volcano, it is clad with myriad glaciers. Its 14,410-foot summit challenges hundreds of climbers annually. More than 300 miles of trails encircle the mountain, offering hiking for all abilities. Mountain goat, elk, bear and deer are seen in the wild flower belt just above the tree line. For more information on this area write to: Superintendent, Mt. Rainier National Park, Longmire, WA 98397.

The 1,400 square mile Olympic National Park is pristine and rugged. More than 600 miles of trails wind through the park, offering hikes from glaciers to perpetually shaded jungles. Dense coniferous rain forests on the west side of the peninsula receive a yearly rainfall of 140 inches, while the northeast side of the peninsula accumulates only inches. Within the rain forests, Douglas fir, Sitka spruce and western hemlock attain astonishing heights and diameters. The park also includes a 60-mile stretch along the Pacific Ocean, where rocky headlands meet charging waves in a resounding natural symphony. For more information write to: Superintendent, Olympic National Park, 600 E. Park Ave., Port Angeles, WA 98362.

The North Cascades National Park encompasses 1,053 square miles of wild alpine meadows, deep glaciated canyons, waterfalls and icefalls, and a string of icy, glacially fed lakes. Twenty-four mile long Ross Lake contains three dams which provide electrical power for Seattle. For information contact: Superintendent, No. Cascades National Park, Sedro Woolley, WA 98284.

Weather

The Cascade Range, running the length of the state, effectively divides Washington into a wet side and a dry side. Statistically, western Washington doesn't get that much rain — about 34 inches annually in the Seattle area (Atlanta, New York and Chicago all get more). Nonetheless, the skies are often grey and there is often drizzle. On the Western side of the Olympic Mountains, rainfall averages a sodden 140 inches a year. After all, that's what makes all those beautiful evergreens grow.

Western Washington has a very mild maritime climate with average summer high temperatures of 65°F and average winter lows of 43°F. It rarely snows in the Puget Sound area. But, in the Cascades, it's another story. The world's record for annual snowfall (more that 93 feet) was set at Paradise on Mount Rainier in the winter of 1971-72.

The eastern side of the Cascades is much warmer in the summer, colder in the winter and drier year-round. Average summer temperature is 66°F, winter is 29 and the average precipitation is only about 13 inches.

Liquor Laws

Legal drinking age in Washington is 21. Liquor is sold by the bottle in state liquor stores, and by the drink in licensed establishments. Beer, wine and liquor are sold by the drink daily from 6 a.m. to 2 a.m.; no package sales are permitted Sundays and holidays.

Driving In Washington

The main south-north route is I-5, which crosses the Columbia River at Portland to enter Washington at Vancouver and continues north through Olympia, Tacoma, Seattle, Everett and Bellingham to the Canadian border. Interstate 90 begins in Seattle, crosses the Cascades and continues across the state to Spokane and the Idaho border. Interstate 82 hugs the eastern slope of the Cascades from Prosser to Ellensburg.

On the west, U.S. 101, a two-lane highway most of the way, enters the state near the mouth of the Columbia River and circles the Olympic Peninsula. U.S. 97 leads through central Oregon and central Washington to the Canadian Border.

The speed limit is 65 mph on rural highways and 55 mph in urban areas, less where posted on secondary roads and in populated areas. All persons in the vehicle must wear a seat belt. Right turns are permitted following a full stop at a red light. Radar is widely used.

This is timber country and, on back roads, you should be especially careful of logging trucks that often swing suddenly around a bend and may want to take their half of the road out of the middle.

Traveling By Washington State Ferry

Seattle's unique maritime flavor is most evident in the ferry system which links the mainland to many of the "bedroom islands" in Puget Sound and the Kitsap Peninsula. Bainbridge Island, just one half-hour ride from downtown Seattle, and Vashon Island, 15 minutes from Fauntleroy, are rural communities with peaceful pastures and charming towns. The ferry ride provides one of the best points to view the sunset over the Olympic Mountains and Seattle's dramatic skyline. The big green-and-white boats carry both passengers and cars. Traveling by car requires a bit more planning as lines tend to form during commuter hours and on weekends and holidays. It is advisable to check the schedule, then plant the car in line well ahead of sailing time. Ferries run frequently during daylight hours and less often at night. Access to the San Juan Islands is provided from Anacortes. A written schedule for all routes may be obtained from Washington State Ferry System, State Ferry Terminal, Seattle, WA 98104. Recorded schedules are available by calling: (206) 464-6400, (800) 542-0810 or (800) 542-7052.

Washington Wineries

The Yakima River Valley and the Columbia River Basin produce premium vinefera grapes. These regions exhibit many similarities to the great wine-growing areas of France in latitude and climate. A fine collection of vintners are located within easy driving distance from Seattle. Their wines are achieving international recognition and taking their place among the great wines of the world. For a map and winery listing, contact: The Enological Society for the Pacific Northwest, 5806 16th N.E., Seattle, WA 98105, (206) 523-4372.

Information Sources For Washington

Washington operates year-round visitor information centers on I-5 at Blaine (Drayton Harbor Mall), Vancouver, and at Sea-Tac International Airport. In summer, they are open on I-90 at the Idaho-Washington border; on U.S. 97 four miles south of the Canadian border; on State Highway 401 one-half mile east of the Astoria bridge; and 14 miles north of Vancouver on I-5. Further information may be obtained by writing or calling:

Tourism Development Division
101 General Administration Bldg.
Olympia, WA 98504
(800) 541-WASH out of state
(800) 544-1800 within Washington

National Park Service
Pacific Northwest Regional Office
Westin Building, Room 1920
2001 Sixth Avenue
Seattle, WA 98121
(206) 442-0170

U.S. Forest Service, Regional Office
P.O. Box 3623
Portland, OR 97208
(503) 221-2877

Washington Department of Fisheries
115 General Administration Building
Olympia, WA 98504
(206) 753-6600

Seattle/King County Convention and Visitors Bureau
1815 Seventh Ave.
Seattle, WA 98119
(206) 447-7273

Washington State Game Department
600 N. Capitol Way
Olympia, WA 98504

Washington State Parks
State Parks and Recreation Commission
P.O. Box 1128
Olympia, WA 98504

San Juan Islands Chamber of Commerce
P.O. Box 98
Friday Harbor, WA 98250
(206) 378-4600

Pacific County Visitor Information
P.O. Box P
South Bend, WA 98586
(206) 875-5224

Central Whidbey Chamber of Commerce
P.O. Box 152
Coupeville, WA 98239
(206) 678-5434

Selected Washington Events

January
National Boat Show — Seattle
Mt. Baker Chili Eruption and Cook Off — Bellingham

February
Bluegrass Jam Session — Darrington
Chinese New Year Celebration — Seattle

March
Whale Watching — Westport
Volksmarch & 10k — Edmonds

April
Skagit Valley Tulip Festival — Mount Vernon Area
Apple Blossom Festival — Wenatchee
Annual Ragtime Rhodie Festival — Long Beach

May
Blessing of the Fleet — Anacortes and Ilwaco
Bloomsday Run (biggest in PNW) — Spokane

June
Sound to Narrows 12k — Tacoma
World's Longest Beach Run — Long Beach Peninsula
Annual Art Show — Oak Harbor

July
Darrington Bluegrass Festival — Darrington
Pacific Northwest Arts & Crafts Festival — Bellevue
Jazz Festival — Friday Harbor

August
Long Beach Rodeo — Long Beach Peninsula
Arts and Crafts Festival — Coupeville
Washington State International Kite Festival — Long Beach Peninsula
Island County Fair — Langley

September
Bumpershoot (Seattle Arts Festival) — Seattle
Washington State International Air Fair — Everett
Western Washington Fair — Puyallup

October
Salmon Days — Issaquah
Grape Harvest and Crush — Yakima

November
Bluegrass Jam Sessions — Darrington
Jazz Festival — Ocean Shores

December
Christmas Ships Parade — Seattle
Yule Log and Christmas Lighting — Poulsbo

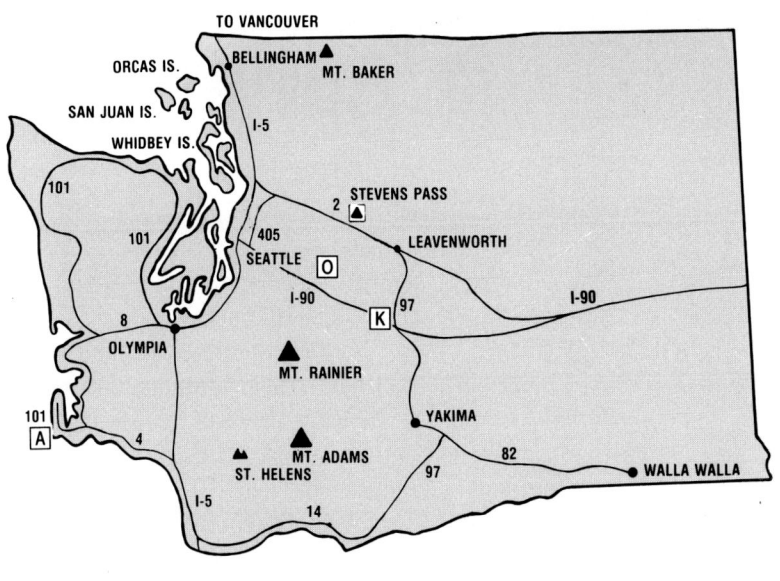

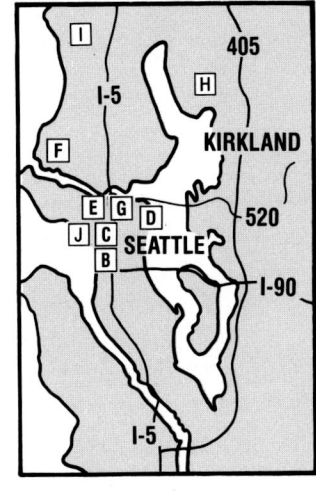

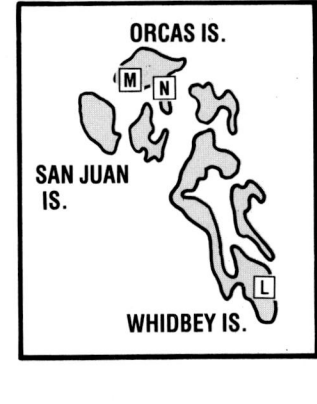

LONG BEACH
- [A] SHELBURNE INN AND SHOALWATER RESTAURANT

SEATTLE
- [B] ALEXIS
- [C] INN AT THE MARKET
- [D] DOMINIQUE'S PLACE
- [E] ADRIATICA
- [F] RAY'S BOATHOUSE
- [G] LAKE UNION AIR
- [H] CAFE JUANITA
- [I] brusseau's
- [J] VICTORIA CLIPPER

CASCADES
- [K] HIGH COUNTRY PACKERS

WHIDBEY ISLAND
- [L] HOME BY THE SEA

ORCAS ISLAND
- [M] TURTLEBACK FARM INN
- [N] CHRISTINA'S

FALL CITY
- [O] HERBFARM

THE SHELBURNE INN HOTEL AND THE SHOALWATER RESTAURANT

Address: (P.O. Box 250), Seaview, WA 98644
Telephone: (206) 642-2442 (inn), (206) 642-4142 (restaurant)
Location: South of Long Beach on Long Beach Peninsula
Hosts: David Campiche and Laurie Anderson, Innkeepers;
    Tony and Ann Kischner, Restaurateurs
Room Rates: $60 to $110 double. Midweek off-season lodging and
    dining packages available October through June
Credit Cards: American Express, MasterCard, Visa
Remarks: Complimentary country breakfast with room. No pets.
Hours: Lunch noon to 2:30 p.m., dinner 5:30 to 9:30 p.m.
    Sunday brunch 9 a.m. to 2:30 p.m.

The first thing you notice upon entering the Shelburne Inn is that the antique clocks have stopped. In fact, looking around the lobby where the turn-of-the-century motif is so thoroughly intact, you might just be tempted to tap your wrist watch and wonder if this is a scene from "Somewhere in Time."

The Shelburne, built in 1896, has just celebrated 90 years of distinguished service. Located on Washington's 28-mile Long Beach Peninsula, the inn was originally a mecca for Oregonians escaping the heat of the city. Summer guests would steam along the river on the paddlewheeler *T.J. Potter* to the Port of Illwaco, then hop a narrow gauge rail to Seaview. The existing structure, now on the National Registry of Historic Places, has undergone a series of changes, including the 1911 uniting of two buildings from opposing sides of the street in the spot where the inn now rests.

David Campiche, a Seaview native, watched the inn deteriorate for several years until he and his wife, Laurie Anderson, decided to purchase it in 1977 and begin renovation. Both were knowledgeable in antiques, and together they scoured England and Holland for the quality pieces now filling the inn. In 1983, a major expansion of the lower level was completed, and Art Nouveau stained glass windows were integrated into the structure. A new wing, built in 1986, added five guest rooms, bringing the total to 17. "It's like a canvas," says David. "We keep working on it until we get it right."

Quiet Victorian Retreat

The three story inn has 17 rooms; ten have private baths. Hand-stitched quilts, crocheted pillow slips, brass bedsteads, and marble-topped dressers add distinction to each room. Impressionist prints and lace curtains add a light touch. A few rooms open onto a veranda where potted geraniums grow.

A couple of large tables in the lobby are set for breakfast. The country style feast is included in the room rate. "Shelburne Eggs" (with sautéed red onion and spinach) is one of three entrée selections that change frequently. David's homemade venison sausage and Laurie's baked goods are other favorites.

The Shoalwater Restaurant is well worth the trip.

First-Rate Dining

The Shoalwater Restaurant shares what owner Tony Kischner describes as a "symbiotic relationship" with the Shelburne Inn. Linked by a couple of doorways, a strong friendship, and a common spirit, the two businesses work in harmony to provide a complete dining and lodging experience. The dining room decor is consistent with that of the inn.

Tony, formerly manager of Seattle's prestigious Other Place, and his wife Ann joined David and Laurie in 1981. Tony blends the best of his international upbringing with his restaurant training to create a superb dining experience. Northwest foods are showcased in a seasonally varied menu. "People travel for miles to have our mussel chowder," he says. Chowder is but one of the masterfully prepared items offered.

Fresh Willapa Bay oysters are featured, both on the half-shell as appetizers, and Cajun style for an entrée. Columbia River white sturgeon in an inventive Oriental marinade is grilled to perfection. Roast Oregon quail is topped with a delicate rosemary, port, walnut and cream cheese sauce; Pacific halibut is stuffed with crab and shrimp, mushrooms and scallions, and served with a light Asiago cheese cream sauce. Ann's homemade bread accompanies the meal, and her dessert tray merits rave reviews.

Lunch and Sunday brunch are of consistent quality, and again utilize fresh ingredients and culinary expertise. Tony is proud of his extensive wine list, and enjoys sharing his recommendations.

The most recent addition to the Shelburne/Shoalwater duo is the Heron & Beaver Pub Lounge. Northwest microbreweries are spotlighted, as are single-

The innkeepers serve a full-course breakfast.

malt Scotch whiskys. The full bar offers an intimate spot for cocktails, or for a meal of light pub fare. Scotch eggs, sausage rolls, and British pasties may be among the offerings served in the cozy gathering place.

Year-Round Destination

A favorite time on the Long Beach Peninsula is winter, when big storms hammer their way along the coast. Bundle up and beachcomb for Japanese fishing floats, driftwood and shells. Drive for miles along the state-owned beach where kite flying and photography are favorite oceanside pastimes. Steelhead fishing is prime in winter, while the summer months bring the salmon to the mouth of the Columbia River. Loomis Lake and others nearby teem with trout and bass. Horseback riding, tennis and golf are all found within easy reach of the inn. Curio shops, museums and art galleries, too, await exploration. The southwest corner of the state is on the bird migration route and tens of thousands of waterfowl and shorebirds are seen skimming the beach.

Long Island rests under the protected arm of the peninsula in Willapa Bay. A 274-acre grove of red cedars is one of the last remaining reproducing climax forests that first sprouted during a dramatic West Coast climate change 4,000 years ago. Cedars reach 11 feet in diameter, and average 150 feet in height. Tours are available to this island, which is also home to elk, geese and heron.

Getting There

From Seattle, take I-5 south to Olympia, then Highway 8 and 12 to Montesano. Follow Highway 101 south to Seaview. From the Oregon coast, follow U.S. 101 across the Astoria bridge and turn left to Illwaco. Head north for two miles until you reach Seaview.

ALEXIS HOTEL SEATTLE

Address: 1007 First Avenue, Seattle, WA 98104
Telephone: (206) 624-4844, (800) 426-7033
outside Washington
Location: Two blocks from the waterfront in downtown Seattle
Room Rates: $135 to $150 double, suites from $150 to $260,
single $115, weekend rates available
Credit Cards: American Express, Carte Blanche, Diners Club,
MasterCard, Visa
Remarks: Children under 12 stay free, rates include Continental
breakfast.

The Alexis Hotel is a luxury hotel of European inspiration. Captivatingly quiet, the downtown Seattle auberge is elegantly simple and simply elegant.

The handsome building housing the hotel was originally a 1901 office building designed by Max Umbrecht for prominent Seattle businessman James W. Clise. It headquartered Clise's firms for about 15 years, but in 1917 he moved on and the Globe Building suffered a six-decade period of decline. The building survived the Depression years as a home to the public market, became a parking garage, and in 1980 became part of a six-square-block area undergoing revitalization by Paul Schell's Cornerstone Development Company. The Alexis, totally renovated by the noted Baumgardner Architects, has earned a place in the National Register of Historic Places.

Service Counts

Elegance and luxury aside, what the Alexis Hotel really stands on is its service. A doorman greets you to park your car while a bellman takes your bags to your room. (Neither expect a tip.) There is sherry in your room when you arrive, and chocolates on your pillow after evening turn-down service. If you leave your shoes outside the door at night they will be returned in the morning, shiny as new, with your choice of newspaper. A concierge and multilingual staff are on hand to assist with any requests you have, from sending a package or telex to sightseeing or dining tips. Limosine service within the downtown area and access to a local health club are available as well.

The Alexis Seattle has 54 rooms in 18 room styles. Parlor suites, executive one-bedroom suites, and fireplace suites are the more spacious. Many rooms overlook the inner courtyard. Some have a jacuzzis, wet bar and refrigerator. Televisions are tucked away in beautiful armoires. Italian and Alaskan marble accent the pastel colors used throughout the hotel. All rooms have extension phones, plush terry robes, fine soaps and lotions, and down pillows. There is a steam room on the third floor, and two lighted tennis courts on the roof. A complimentary continental breakfast of warm croissants, fresh fruits and jams and coffee will be delivered to your room upon request.

Room service is available 24 hours a day.

Alexis Style Dining

The Alexis Hotel Seattle opened their own Cafe Alexis in the manner they know best: small, polished and perfect in detail, yet gracious, warm and welcoming. The restaurant seats 28 in its intimate room. Rotating exhibits by Northwest artists grace the walls. The menu changes weekly; specials change daily. International flavors are added to traditional dishes, mixed with Northwest freshness, and served simply and beautifully.

The Bookstore ... A Bar offers cocktail service as well as light lunches and innovative appetizers. Housed in a former bookstore, it features micro-brewery beers and hot, soft pretzels. It is a friendly place where regulars are known by name and not-so-regulars are easily engaged in conversation. International newspapers, magazines and books are available for browsing or for purchase. After all, it is a bookstore . . . and a bar.

Seattle's Heart

The Alexis Seattle is located near the center of a vital metropolis. The business and financial district is only blocks away, as are the airline office and governmental centers. The world famous Pike Place Market is a short walk away near the busy waterfront area.

Head south from the front door of the hotel to reach Pioneer Square, the heart of Seattle's historic district. The area had its beginnings in 1852, and many of the old brick buildings have been restored to their original state. Shops, restaurants, exotic boutiques and art galleries now occupy the handsome structures. The Underground Tour takes you under present-day Pioneer Square for a glimpse of Seattle in the 1890s, before a devastating fire burned

The intimate Cafe Alexis is just off the lobby.

it to the ground. The southern border of the Pioneer Square district is the Kingdome, where many of Seattle's major sporting events are held. Nearby is the hub of the Asian community, the International District, where dozens of ethnic shops and restaurants line the streets.

Just as Pioneer Square is Seattle's historic heart, the Seattle Center is its cultural heart. The 74-acre legacy of the 1962 World's Fair is site of the 605-foot Space Needle, Seattle's most distinctive landmark. An elevator swiftly carries passengers to the observation level from which a 360-degree view of the city and environs can be seen. Both mountain ranges, the Cascades to the east and Olympics to the west, Puget Sound, Lake Washington and Lake Union, and the myriad of bridges, parks and barges may be seen from this bird's-eye view. The restaurant, one level below, revolves one full turn per hour, so while you dine there is an ever-changing mural of sights.

The Center grounds hold the Pacific Science Center, with its hands-on displays, the Imax Theater and laser shows. The Bagley Wright Theater is home to Seattle's repertory company which has a six-play season from October to April. The Opera House is host to programs by the Seattle Symphony, Pacific Northwest Ballet and Seattle Opera.

Getting There

From northbound I-5,take the Madison Stree Exit. Head west on Madison to 1st Avenue. From southbound I-5, take the Stewart Steet Exit to 1st Avenue. Turn left and continue to Madison. The hotel is on the corner of 1st and Madison. Valet parking is available for $8 per day.

■ DOMINIQUE'S PLACE

Address:	1927 43rd Avenue East, Seattle, WA 98112
Telephone:	(206) 329-6620
Hosts:	Dominique and Chou Chou Place
Cuisine:	French
Prices:	$5.75 to $15 for lunch crepes and entrees, dinner entrees $11.50 to $22, five-course dinner $32.
Credit Cards:	American Express, Diners Club, MasterCard, Visa, Discover
Hours:	Lunch Monday through Friday 11:30 a.m. to 2:30 p.m. (summertime only), dinner 5 to 10:30 p.m., until 11:30 p.m. Friday and Saturday

"The secret to sauces is fullness of flavor," says owner Dominique Place. "Making sauces is very much like making a fine wine." Dominique's sensitive approach to sauces is but one reason his restaurant is a rare dining find.

French born Dominique Place received extensive culinary training in France. Early in his career he accumulated an impressive collection of awards and distinctions, making it clear he was destined to be a skillful chef. A Seattle restaurateur discovered Dominique and brought him to work in the States. Dominique later opened his own restaurant in what had been Madison Park's Crepe de Paris. His wife Chou Chou manages the books.

The small bistro is snuggled into a corner of this chic Seattle neighborhood. Neighbored by boutiques, flower shops and fine gift stores, it gazes directly out onto Lake Washington and beyond to the Cascade Mountains. In summer, linen cloaked tables line the sidewalk under the restaurant's blue canvas awnings. In winter, steaming windows tell of cozy evenings inside by the fire. In any season, Dominique's fare is of consistently fine quality.

■ Fresh and Varied

Dominique makes several trips per week to the local markets in search of fresh ingredients. His menu reflects seasonal variations as well as his own personal taste. He designs four- and five-course menus which change frequently. These *prix fixe* meals showcase a well-rounded variety of specialties. The five-course meal typically begins with an appetizer; for instance, sautéed rabbit liver with a light raspberry sauce, or salmon and smoked salmon paté with a light herb dressing. A salad selection follows: mixed green with marinated scallops, prawns and geoduck; or spinach and lettuce with bacon, mushrooms and goat cheese dressing. A palate cleanser of champagne and fruit ice is next, followed by a choice of three or four entrées such as roasted squab with persimmon sauce, sautéed duck breast with pear and ginger sauce, veal escalope with lime sauce, or fresh fish braised with olive oil. A Grand Dessert Maison, "chef's fantasy," caps off the meal.

Dominique's à la carte menu offers unique selections. Lamb rack medallions served with a rosemary cream and mustard seed sauce falls at the higher end of the price scale, while crepes filled with chicken fillets and vegetables in plum sauce hits the lower range. Full-meal salads, soups, and a plate of cheeses are among the à la carte choices. Crepes are a specialty here, and are served in a number of ways. An exotic flambé of raspberries, chocolate, and ice cream crepes is the perfect end to a satisfying meal.

Lunches consist of a slimmed down version of the dinner menu. A light salmon with sorrel sauce is always a favorite, as is a mixed green salad with orange and praline dressing and sweetbreads. French onion soup or soup du jour make great accompaniments to the salad or can serve as an entire meal. Fresh bread from one of Seattle's fine French bakeries is delivered daily to complement the meals.

An extensive wine list offers selections designed to enhance the meal. French and California wines dominate the cellars.

Getting There

Heading north on I-5, take the Madison Avenue Exit in downtown Seattle and continue east until it ends on the shore of Lake Washington. Dominique's is one building down from the corner of 43rd and Madison. Heading sout on I-5, take the Bellevue/Kirland Exit (520) to the Montlake Exit. At the light go straight along 520 on Washington Boulevard. Go through Arboretum until you reach Madison Avenue. Take left on Madison and continue to Lake Washington. Dominique's is across the street from Madison Park beach.

Dominique's is Seattle's version of a French auberge.

THE INN AT THE MARKET

Address: 86 Pine Street, Seattle, WA 98101
Telephone: (206) 443-3600, (800) 446-4484 (outside of Seattle)
Location: Downtown, in Pike Place Market
Room Rates: $75 to $140 double; suites from $155, $15 for each
               additional person, lower rates on weekends
Credit Cards: American Express, Carte Blanche, MasterCard, Visa,
               JB, Discover
Remarks: Children under 16 stay free in parents' room,
               nonsmoking rooms available

Throw open your windows. Savor the heady aromas of coffee, cheese and spices wafting up from the Pike Place Market. Listen to the sonorous *hoot hoot* as the ferry from Bainbridge Island noses into its dock on the waterfront. Gaze westward across Elliott Bay and soak in the last rays of an orange sun silhouetting the jagged peaks of the Olympic Mountains. These, and more, are part of the sensory extravaganza that will be part of your stay at Seattle's Inn at the Market.

Uniquely Seattle

The Inn at the Market offers a unique experience. Its location in the middle of the vital original public market is a much-coveted spot. This neighborhood hotel, one which will feel like home, is conveniently situated in a thriving portion of a large city.

The inn is a small hotel with big ideas. Like complimentary limosine service to the downtown area. Small refrigerators stocked with a selection of beverages. Evening turndown and a supply of coffee and tea to be brewed in your room, at your leisure. A basket of market-selected amenities awaits in the spacious, tiled bathrooms. For the health conscious, a full-service health club offered to guests at a nominal charge is just one block away.

Of the 65 guest rooms, 58 offer a view of Puget Sound, the Olympic Mountains, the garden courtyard or the market itself. Three parlor suites on the northwest corner offer the best vantage points. All rooms have floor to ceiling bay windows that open. One-bedroom suites can be converted into two-bedroom townhouses with parlor and connecting bedroom on one level, and second bedroom upstairs.

The lobby is decorated with antiques, overstuffed furniture, fresh floral arrangements, and a fire glowing in the brick fireplace. A fifth-floor rooftop deck offers a 180-degree view of Mount Rainier, Elliott Bay and the Pike Place Market below.

The lobby is furnished in a country decor.

Conference and reception rooms are available for groups. Intimate meal functions can accommodate up to 40, while grand rooftop receptions can handle 150-175 guests.

In the Inn

Select shops and services front the Inn's courtyard. The Comfort Zone Relaxation Spa offers massage therapy, whirlpool, float tank and suntanning, all of which may be billed to your room. The Gravity Bar offers healthy and exotic food and juices created from the market's fresh produce. Baked goods, fresh fruits, granola, warm cereals, and a creative "Eggs Crescent" are available. Another true Seattle treasure is found in the Inn — Cafe Dilettante. The famed chocolaterie provides speciality soups and sandwiches, espresso and desserts. A wine bar features Northwest wines as well as champagnes from around the world.

A Little Village

Stepping out the door of the Inn at the Market, one has the sense of being in a small village. Pike Place Market is an old-time farmer's market where you stroll past fresh fish stalls, vegetable stands and delicatessens amid a chorus of voices calling out in a dozen languages. In 1971 the market was saved from the wrecking ball and became the focus of the Pike Place Market Historic District, a seven-acre area that has become the symbolic heart of Seattle.

Seattle on Foot and Afloat

The Inn is ideally situated for shopping or exploring downtown Seattle on foot. From the shops around the market to the major downtown boutiques and

Many of the rooms overlook Elliott Bay and the Pike Place Market.

department stores, it is only six blocks. Business travelers will find Seattle's major office buildings a short walk away as well. The symphony, repertory theater, opera and ballet are all easily accessible. A movie theater in the market shows foreign and local films. A corner newsstand sells tabloids in several languages and magazines on most any subject imaginable. Neighboring art galleries display a variety of local and imported talent.

Descending the stairs from the market, known as the Pike Hill Climb, you will arrive on Seattle's waterfront. Seafood restaurants, marine supply stores, import stores, the Seattle Aquarium and Omni Dome Theater line the busy wharfs. A tramway runs parallel to the water, offering easy access to the entire length of the district. Harbor tours are available from a number of operators along these piers.

Washington State is proud of its unique ferry system. Passengers and cars travel across Elliott Bay and Puget Sound to the "bedroom islands" of Bainbridge and Vashon, and to the mainland port of Bremerton. Take a ride from Pier 56 to Winslow, on Bainbridge Island, for a half-hour cruise. Winslow offers a fine selection of shops and restaurants, and makes a pleasant afternoon or evening jaunt. Most Seattlites agree, there are few better spots from which to view the sunset over the Olympic Mountains than from the sundeck of the ferry.

Getting There

Follow First Avenue through downtown Seattle to either Pike Street or Stewart Street. You may enter the hotel from either one. Parking under the Inn at the Market may be limited, but there are several fee lots within a block of the hotel where long term parking is available.

ADRIATICA

Address:	1107 Dexter North, Seattle, WA 98109
Telephone:	(206) 285-5000
Hosts:	Jim and Connie Malevitsis, Owners and Managers
Cuisine:	Mediterranean
Prices:	Entrees $11 to $17
Credit Cards:	American Express, MasterCard, Visa
Hours:	Sunday through Thursday 5:30 to 10 p.m., Friday and Saturday until 11 p.m.; bar is open 5 p.m. to 1 a.m. Sunday through Thursday, until 2 a.m. on Friday and Saturday

Adriatica is located in a remodeled 1920s stucco and clapboard house on a cliff above the south end of Seattle's Lake Union. The Mediterranean restaurant's Greek owner and maitre d' Jim Malevitsis came to this country over 30 years ago. The authentic atmosphere and cuisine belie his European origins. With his wife Connie, who handles the books and menu planning, Jim created the restaurant out of a love for good ethnic cuisine.

The kitchen occupies the first floor of the three story restaurant; the dining room is on the second. The bar on the third floor provides the most dramatic view. Full course meals are served in the dining room, while the bar features a selection of appetizers and light suppers. The outside deck is a popular gathering spot in warm weather.

The main dining room is divided into small, cozy rooms carpeted in "Adriatic blue." Jim's photographs of European scenes and original Greek watercolors set a Mediterranean theme, while white linens and candlelight lend a romantic tone to the warm atmosphere.

L'Heure Bleue

"My favorite time here is what the French call 'l'heure bleue'," Jim. said "At dusk the lights are coming on around Lake Union, and there is a special quality to the natural light." Little wonder this is his favorite time. As the sun eases down, a play of lights and shadows on the lake create an ever-changing panorama. Sailboats and windsurfers slice through the diamond-shaped patterns of light, and city neon blues, reds and yellows dance across the water.

Mediterranean Cuisine

Chef Nancy Flume prepares an array of seafoods and traditional Mediterranean dishes utilizing only the highest quality ingredients. Two or three fresh seafood items are served nightly: white king salmon, halibut and petrale sole are grilled with garlic, olive oil, lemon juice and white wine. Seafood souvlaki (grilled prawns and scallops), is basted with cumin, lime and red chile butter.

Meat entrées include raznijici (lamb marinated in zinfandel wine with rosemary and garlic), and filet mignon basted with rosemary, Marsala and garlic butter. Chargrilled New York steak with a peppercorn, shallot butter sauce is a new twist to the traditional entrée. A favorite pasta dish is pensotti (large ravioli) filled with spinach, chard and ricotta topped with a walnut sauce.

Traditional Greek salads such as Horiatiki (a Greek village salad with cucumber, tomato, feta, Greek olives and peppers) or a special Belgian endive salad with toasted walnuts, Roquefort and cilantro make a nice accompaniment to the meal.

A selection of desserts such as chocolate decadence with raspberry sauce or ricotta mouse with chocolate and brandy are the perfect finale to the meal. A fully stocked wine cellar is sure to please most tastes.

Many guests elect to make a full meal of appetizers in the bar. Roasted whole garlic served with croutons and goat cheese is a signature dish, and prawns Constantina, with hints of Cajun influence, is another unique offering.

Getting There

From I-5 take the Mercer Street Exit. Follow signs to Seattle Center, cross Westlake, turn right on Roy. Continue two blocks to Dexter, then turn right on Dexter. The restaurant is three blocks north on the left. From downtown go north on 4th or 6th avenues to Denny. Turn right on Denny, then left on Dexter. The restaurant is nine blocks north on the left side. Parking is available on the south side of the restaurant.

Dine overlooking the waters of Lake Union.

THE VICTORIA CLIPPER

Address: 2701 Alaskan Way, Pier 69, Seattle, WA 98121
Telephone: Seattle (206) 448-5000; Victoria (604) 382-8100
Location: Departs Pier 69 in Seattle; Fast Ferry Terminal
                       in Victoria
Host: Darrell Bryan, General Manager
Rates: May 16 to September 13: one way $35; round trip
                       $59. September 14 to May 15: one way $29; round
                       trip $49. Child, senior citizen, or group rates
                       available. Rates and schedule subject to change
                       without notice.
Credit Cards: Visa, MasterCard, American Express
Remarks: The Clipper makes two round trips daily May 1 to
                       September 30.

Referred to as the "Concorde of the Seas," the double-hulled Victoria Clipper is the quickest, most convenient water link between Seattle and Victoria, B.C. This 300-passenger Norwegian-built water-jet catamaran whisks passengers between these two delightful cities daily, year-round, on a pleasurable, two and one-half hour journey. Christened in Bergen, Norway (Seattle's sister city) in April, 1986, the 130-foot Victoria Clipper was fully operational by July 1 of the same year.

The two passenger levels on the Clipper provide comfortable airline-style seating with plenty of leg room. The lower level offers smoking and non-smoking sections; the upper is non-smoking only. The views from both are picture-window perfect. Passengers are free to wander about the vessel as it cruises at a smooth 32 knots. An outdoor deck is available for taking in the fresh marine air and viewing the surrounding islands and waterways. The Victoria Clipper gracefully plies the waters of Admiralty Inlet and the Strait of Juan de Fuca, passing islands and inlets on its 71-mile route. It is not uncommon to spot Dahl porpoises, whales, seals, and a variety of sea and land birds en route. The bridge is enclosed in glass, exposing the sophisticated navigational equipment inside for viewing. Occasionally, passengers are invited to visit the bridge after the Clipper docks.

The multilingual staff includes the Chief Engineer, Mate, Master and five attendants. All provide cheerful, efficient service. The vessel's personnel have had extensive training on the Victoria Clipper as well as many years of other personal nautical experience. A selection of snacks and drinks, as well as alcoholic beverages, may be ordered from the attendants. Menu items include a Continental Breakfast Basket (muffin, mini-bagel with cream cheese, jam and a tangerine) and a Light Supper Basket (Northwest smoked salmon, mini-bagel with cream cheese, cheddar cheese, crackers, bread sticks and an apple). Both include tea or coffee. A small gift shop on board is stocked with items such as Clipper t-shirts and hats, film and playing cards. A limited selection of perfumes and duty-free liquor is available for approximately 30 to 50% discount.

Package Deals

The helpful cruise director is on board to assist with passengers' arrangements in Victoria or Seattle. The ship is equipped with a VectorOne phone which the cruise director uses to secure lodging, restaurant or rental car reservations. Grayline tour packages can also be booked on board, as well as shuttle transfer to downtown Victoria for a minimal fee.

Seasonally, several one- and two-night packages are available in Victoria or Seattle. These can be booked when you make your Clipper reservation, or once you are on board, depending upon availability. These deluxe accommodations include Special Places' inns, cab transfers or rental cars. A special joint fare is available utilizing the Clipper and Lake Union Air.

Customs and Baggage

Upon arrival in Victoria or Seattle, all passengers must clear customs. Citizens of the U.S. and Canada must carry proof of citizenship when entering a foreign port. Passengers from other countries will need a passport or visa. The luggage allowance on the victoria Clipper is two bags per person. these are checked upon boarding, then retrieved prior to clearing customs. Materials required during the trip should be carried in a small bag on board the vessel.

Getting There

Seattle's Pier 69 is located along Alaskan Way at the foot of Broad Street. Victoria's Ogden Point terminal is one mile from downtown on Dallas Road.

The sea level way to travel from Seattle to Victoria, B.C.

LAKE UNION AIR

Address: 1100 Westlake Avenue North, Seattle, WA 98109
Telephone: (206) 284-0300
Location: On Southwest bank of Lake Union in Seattle
Host: Clyde Carlson, Owner and Operator
Credit Cards: American Express, MasterCard, Visa

The quickest and most comfortable way to reach many of the special places mentioned in this book is by float plane. If you are traveling to the San Juans or Canada, flying can save you a long day on the road or ferry. If you arrive at the Seattle-Tacoma airport on one of the major commercial carriers, a quick, no hassle connection with Lake Union Air can save you both time and effort.

Lake Union Air is owned and operated by Clyde Carlson. The airline utilizes single-engine float planes, including four five-passenger Cessna 206s and five seven-passenger De Havilland Beavers. Lake Union Air has regularly scheduled year-round service to the San Juans and Victoria, but, according to Carlson," We'll fly anywhere there's water to land on."

Born and raised in Seattle, Carlson began taking flying lessons at Boeing Field back in 1968. He became a flight instructor and charter pilot for Lake Union Air in the 1970s. In 1976 Carlson bought a five-passenger Cessna 206 and moved to southeast Alaska, where his operation expanded from one plane to five in only five years. He then returned to Seattle with his five Cessna 206s and purchased Lake Union Air in 1981 with the intention of turning it into a scheduled seaplane operation. "I've always wanted to fly," says Carlson. "I love sharing this area with others." Clyde's sharing with others has helped to build the airline into one of the most active and respected small carriers in the Pacific Northwest.

Clyde's staff willingly shares their knowledge of the area with passengers. As the plane soars along, the pilot points out various landmarks and geographical formations. The planes' large windows allow prime viewing of the Olympic and Cascade Mountains, of small towns and urban areas, and of the many waterways below. Often, whales, deer and elk are spotted form the plane. Polite and courteous, the pilots make the trip fun for even the most timid of flyers.

Anywhere There's Water

Lake Union Air has year-round regularly scheduled service to Victoria's Inner Harbour ($48 one way, $90 round trip), Friday Harbor and Roche Harbor on San Juan Island, Fisherman's Bay on Lopez Island, Rosario on Orcas Island, Decatur and West Sound.

The North Coast

Regular, seasonal service is also available to Desolation Sound, Campbell River, April Point, Blind Channel, Greenway Sound, Stuart Island and other points in British Columbia. Northbound flights to British Columbia clear customs at Victoria (if that is your destination) or at Nanaimo. You pass through U.S. customs at Lake Union on your return. (Remember to check with the customs office for restrictions on fruits and vegetables transported into Canada. This will save delays in clearing customs.

You are permitted 25 pounds of baggage; baggage over 25 pounds will be carried if space is available, but space is often limited. With advance reservations, the airline will pick you up and deliver you to Sea-Tac airport at no extra charge. For those who drive, parking is free at Lake Union Air. Don't forget to keep your camera handy for some spectacular aerial pictures.

Lake Union also offers 30-minute scenic flightseeing trips over Seattle, past the Space Needle, Elliott Bay, Hiram Chittenden Locks, Shilshole Bay, downtown and the Kingdome for $25 per person. With Seattle's varied and beautiful terrain, it is an ideal way to entertain out-of-town guests.

Getting There

From North or South I-5, take the Mercer Street Exit and head west to Fairview Avenue. Turn right, head toward Lake Union, and continue to Westlake. Turn left on Westlake and follow the curve of the lake for one-quarter mile to Lake Union Air, which is on your right.

Enjoy a bird's-eye view of the Pacific Northwest.

RAY'S BOATHOUSE

Address: 6049 Seaview Avenue Northwest, Seattle, WA 98107
Telephone: (206) 789-3770
Cuisine: Seafood
Prices: Lunch $4.95 to $8.95, dinner $11.95 to $21.50
Credit Cards: American Express, Carte Blanche, Diners Club,
                  MasterCard, Visa
Hours: Downstairs dining room 11:30 a.m. to 2:30 p.m. and
                  5 to 10 p.m.; upstairs cafe 11:30 a.m. to 1 a.m.
Remarks: Reservations required in summer.

Ray's Boathouse, located on a spacious Shilshole Bay dock in the Seattle suburb of Ballard, overlooks the entrance to the ship canal that links Lake Union to Puget Sound. This ideal spot affords spectacular views of the parade of pleasure and working boats that funnel into the narrow inlet. Through Ray's floor-to-ceiling windows, diners can gaze across the water to Bainbridge Island and the layers of snow-peaked Olympic Mountains beyond. In addition to its spectacular view, Ray's is widely recognized as one of Seattle's premier seafood restaurants.

Ray's dock was originally used for precisely what the name implies — a boathouse. "Old Ray's" served doughnuts and coffee, and rented a fleet of small fishing boats. In 1973, the present owners bought the dock and heavily remodeled the decrepit structure. Today's clapboard building bears little resemblance to its predecessor, yet the bold red sign pays homage to its forebearer, spelling out RAYS in enormous neon lights.

Ray's is a bi-level restaurant with two personalities. Upstairs, Ray's sparks with convivial ambiance. It is light, bright and airy with skylights above and French doors leading to a waterside deck. The menu is light, emphasizing hors d'oeuvres, small entrées and salads. Tortellini tossed with proscuitto and peas or a bowl of steaming mussels are popular cafe fare. Upstairs at Ray's is a well-known gathering place, particularly on sunny days when nothing will do but to meet for a cocktail outside.

Ray's main floor has one of the most highly regarded dining rooms in Seattle. Intimate, partitioned nooks offer more private dining, while smaller tables line the bank of windows. Polished oak tables sit under low-hanging copper shaded lamps that allow for glare-free viewing of the night lights outside.

A Feast With a View

While the view from Ray's is outstanding, what the restaurant's reputation is really based on is its Northwest seafood cuisine. Chef Wayne Ludvigsen is distinguished as one of the most knowledgeable authorities on fish in the city.

His creations enhance, rather than mask, the fish's natural flavors. An insert in the menu highlights the daily specials: black cod in sake kasu is one of the chef's favorites. To prepare the fish he cures it in salt, marinates it in sake kasu, then grills it over mesquite. Halibut with herb butter, Alaskan king crab legs, shrimp-stuffed artichoke, and Ray's prawns (halved and baked with fresh garlic) are also among the selections. Copper River salmon and Columbia River sturgeon share top billing on the daily sheet.

While seafood is the emphasis, non-seafood entrées, such as grilled filet of tenderloin, are prepared with equal care. Meals are accompanied by crisp vegetables and a small loaf of crusty bread. Ray's wine list is impressive, with more than 300 different items, primarily French, California and Northwest vintages. Quality imported and domestic beers are also available.

The lunch entrées are an abbreviated version of the dinner menu. "Teriyaki Neah Bay Ling Cod," Ray's famous clam chowder, salads and seafood paté, are among the selections offered.

Note: At the time of this writing, Ray's had just endured a severe fire. Plans call for a re-opening in early 1988, at which time the spirit of Ray's, as well as the actual structure, will carry on.

Getting There

From I-5 take the 85th Street Exit and follow it several miles to the end. Veer right, and follow the winding road down to Seaview Avenue. Turn left and head straight for one mile to Ray's. Valet parking is available.

At Ray's you dine center stage for a spectacular view of the Olympic Mountains .

CAFE JUANITA

Address:	9702 Northeast 120th Place, Kirkland, WA 98034
Telephone:	(206) 823-1505
Host:	Peter Dow, Owner
Cuisine:	Italian
Prices:	Entrees $9.75 to $15.50.
Credit Cards:	MasterCard, Visa
Hours:	6 p.m. to 10 p.m. daily.
Remarks:	Reservations suggested

Peter Dow describes himself as a "closet Italian." He is, in fact, owner of one of the Pacific Northwest's finest Italian restaurants — Cafe Juanita. Peter is also chief wine maker for the house label "Cavatappi," which is produced in his full-scale on-premises winery and served only in the restaurant.

Natural Setting

Cafe Juanita is situated in the small community of Juanita, near the northeastern tip of Lake Washington. Formerly a modest brick home, the restaurant is enveloped by willow, maple, and blue spruce trees. The natural setting is carried out inside as well, with muted lighting and warm beige tones set against a hardwood floor. The look is simple and subtle, leaving the fanfare to the food and wine.

Buon Appetito

Unobtrusive chalkboards list the ever-changing list of entrées. Before you've reached the third item, someone is at your table to recite the menu in detail, taking time to colorfully describe each dish. Cafe Juanita's innovative offerings proudly exploit seasonal foods. "We emphasize the freshness of our product," says Peter.

Begin with an appetizer such as steamed mussels or fresh scallops in white wine, garlic and herbs; puntenesca (sun dried tomatoes, olives, capers and garlic over a delicate penne pasta); bresaola (thinly sliced air-dried beef with virgin olive oil and pepper), smoked salmon on the spaghettini made fresh at the Cafe daily.

Cafe Juanita offers eight to ten entrées nightly. A fresh fish selection, such as ahi or swordfish grilled with leeks, lemon, and garlic, is generally available. Other entrées include pollo ai pistacchi (chicken breast baked with proscuitto and parmesan in a pistacchio cream sauce) or piccioni (squab stuffed with Italian sausage and veal in a red wine and tomato sauce). Meat selections may be maiale arrosto (pork loin chops marinated in garlic, olive oil, juniper berries and rosemary), or lasagne (Italian sausage, spinach, and red sauce).

Entrées are followed by a dessert cart featuring homemade specialities, port and liqueurs. Cafe Juanita's own machine churns out fresh fruit gelatos.

Beneath the wisteria in the back yard, Cafe Juanita has a small patio. On summer weekend evenings, Peter may host a special outdoor barbeque. He won't know until that day if the weather is suitable, and recommends calling for a reservation — the patio holds only five tables.

A Focus on Wine

Peter's "Cavatappi" production is reaching 500 cases per year. Known primarily for his sauvignon blanc, this year Peter is introducing the first Italian nebbiolo grown in Washington. He also bottles a small amount of muscat canelli, his special dessert wine. Cafe Juanita also stocks more than 250 Italian wines. This prodigious cellar won an award from *Wine Spectator* as "One of the greatest wine lists in America."

In summer, a cocktail may be enjoyed outside. In winter, a cozy downstairs area is well suited for a pre-dinner glass of wine, or a post-dinner coffee.

Getting There

From Interstate 405 northbound, take Exit 20A and head west on Northeast 116th Street. In approximately two miles, you will reach the main intersection of Juanita (116th and 98th Avenue Northeast). Continue through the intersection one more block to 97th and turn right. The restaurant is one block straight ahead on the left.

The cafe is the only restaurant in the state to make its own house wine.

THE HERBFARM

Address: 32804 Issaquah-Fall City Road, Fall City, WA 98024
Telephone: (206) 784-2222 or (206) 222-7103
Hosts: Lola, Bill and Ron Zimmerman and Carrie Van Dyck
Hours: 9 a.m. to 5 p.m. daily April through October
(weekends open until 6 p.m.). Open Thursday
through Sunday October through Christmas, then
Saturday and Sunday noon to 4 p.m. until April.
Prices: Luncheon program $17.95 per person.
Classes free to $20.
Remarks: Reservations required for luncheon. Free class
schedule and catalog.

Thirty miles east of Seattle, just outside Issaquah, on five fertile acres between the Snoqualmie and Raging rivers, sits the secluded Herbfarm. Two cultivated acres nurture over 400 varieties of herbs and 150 succulents and sedums. An aromatic country store displays dried wreaths, herb books, herb oils and soaps, dried herbs, herb seeds, herb teas, and herb plants.

The Herbfarm began as Lola Zimmerman's hobby over a decade ago. Lola, who enjoyed growing herbs, parked a wheelbarrow full of plants by her driveway, left a Mason jar for quarters, and was soon in business. Her husband Bill retired and lent his own green thumb to the project. The Herbfarm now thrives under the direction of their son Ron and his wife Carrie.

Begin with the Herbfarm tour through the collection of 16 walk-through "theme" gardens. The "Herbal Identification Garden" resembles one that may already be created in your own home, and the tour guide provides helpful hints on the cultivation of herbs. The "Shakespeare's Gardens" signs denote herb-related quotes from the famed bard. The "Good Cooks Garden" entices one to try fresh and different herbs in home cooking. Mints and delicately scented flowers comprise the "Fragrance Garden," where you'll find yourself nose-diving into the aromatic plants. New gardens include the "Shade Garden" (a Northwest necessity); "Herbal Tea Garden" (for refreshment and medicinal purposes); and "Things with Wings" (to attract hummingbirds and butter-flies). The guide, bedecked in an apron reading "Squeeze me, I'm Allspice and Lovage" terminates the tour in the "Garden of Thyme" with the irresistible phrase "It's thyme for lunch."

Next, the group moves inside to a small room where lattice-covered skylights supply filtered light somewhat like a terrarium. Tables are set with crocheted mats and "cabbage leaf" plates. Behind the tiled counter, Ron Zimmerman and Bill Kraut are busy preparing the day's lunch. A menu is tucked in each carefully folded napkin, providing a "culinary road map" to the six-course meal. As the two-hour extravaganza progresses, Ron and Bill interject bits of herblore, share culinary expertise, and generously devulge their recipes. Carrie weaves through the tables with potted herbs for pinching and tasting.

Fresh From the Garden Luncheon

Lunch begins with a refreshing "Herbfarm Haymakers' Switchel," a cool, non-alcoholic drink of New England Shaker origin. The meal that follows is a delightful intermingling of fresh herbs, vegetables raised at the farm, and seasonal seafood, lamb, game or fowl. The menu's theme changes frequently to reflect seasonal variations. A prelude of sea scallop mousse with salmon caviar and dill may be followed by asparagus soup garnished with five varieties of wild mushrooms. An intermezzo of palate-clearing rose geranium ice leads into the salmon with lemon verbena sauce, followed by Salad from the Meadow's Edge — a medley of over 30 herbs, edible flowers and greens.

The day's feast might culminate with Lovage ice cream with purple sage sauce, hot Norfolk punch (a non-alcoholic drink from a 1902 Benedictine monk recipe), coffee and herbal teas. A maximum of 24 are served Friday, Saturday and Sunday and reservations are necessary.

The Herbfarm offers more than 150 classes per year in garden planning, garden care, medicinal herbs, herbal and gourmet cooking, mushroom hunting, and basket weaving.

Getting There

Take Interstate 90 east from Seattle to Exit 22 (Preston-Fall City). Go left across the freeway, then right (Highway 203) through Preston toward Fall City for 3.2 miles. Go left over the green bridge onto 328th S.E. After one-half mile, you will reach a stop sign. The Herbfarm is across the street.

The Herbfarm offers fine food, shopping and more than 150 classes.

brusseau's in edmonds

Address: Fifth and Dayton, Edmonds, WA 98020
Telephone: (206) 774-4166
Host: Jerilyn Brusseau
Cuisine: Northwest regional
Prices: Breakfast $1 to $3.95, lunch $2.90 to $5.75
Credit Cards: MasterCard, Visa
Hours: Monday through Friday 7 a.m. to 6 p.m., Saturday 8 a.m. to 6 p.m., Sunday 8 a.m. to 4 p.m. in winter; one hour later in summer; open for breakfast and lunch only

brusseau's is located in Edmonds, the fashionable town brushing Seattle's northern fringe. It is a daytime place where the early morning air is scented with irresistible aromas from brusseau's own bakery. Local business people know to gather here for morning coffee and the sumptuous selection of baked goods from extra-sour baguettes to pear butter almond swirls. The cafe is also a lunchtime spot where people meet under bright Cinzano umbrellas for a sidewalk picnic, or around cozy tables inside for a warm, leisurely meal. On weekends, brusseau's is a brunch spot. Regulars congregate here weekly, but first timers feel just as welcome.

Country floral wallpaper wraps the dining area in peach and ivory tones that are mirrored in the woven tablecloths. Straw flower arrangements grace each table. Local artists' work and grapevine wreaths augment the homey feeling. Baroque music gently rides the conversational murmurings.

Fresh and Local

Jerilyn Brusseau, owner and cook, is acclaimed as one of the Northwest's finest restaurateurs. Devoted to innovative preparation of fresh local foods, Jerilyn's philosophy is to promote the farmer and educate the people about the foods they eat. She works diligently to carry out her beliefs, foraging ingredients from many sources in the Northwest. Local honey, Canadian hard pear and apple cider, fresh wild mushrooms, microbrewery beer, and fresh churned butter are among her finds. Fruits and vegetables are harvested from Northwest farms, and jams and jellies are prepared by Jerilyn's father, Grandpa Cheney. As the menu says, "Everything at brusseau's is created to nourish not only the body but the mind and the spirit as well."

Bakery and More

brusseau's bakery produces a selection of breads (including the popular seven grain nutrient), bagels and rolls. Wild huckleberry lemon rolls and apple carrot banana bran muffins share the bakery case with a selection of cream cheese swirls, buttery croissants and farmhouse cookies, as well as cakes, pies and cobblers. "Chocolate Decadence" and famous cheesecakes are among the daily dessert selections.

Breakfast specialties include French toast with Vermont maple syrup, ham and cheese croissants, and cream cheese scrambled eggs. Homemade quiches (savory Lorraine or a daily Northwest vegetable quiche) are found on the breakfast and lunch menus. Weekend breakfast is often accompanied by music performed by a local artist.

Lunch entrées and soups change daily, and are listed on a hanging chalkboard. Homemade soups such as "Duchess Vegetarian" warm a wintery day, while fresh salads are favorites any season. Roast turkey salad with hazelnuts, and the Idaho wild and brown rice salad with Oregon shrimp and light herb vinaigrette are among the salad selections. Lighter lunches feature fresh fruits and cheeses, and an array of sandwiches (smoked salmon on sourdough, French or Canadian ham and Lappi Swiss cheese) feed a healthy appetite.

Jerilyn's son, Jeffrey, and daughter, Mari, join the cheerful, dependable staff and handle brusseau's catering, including weddings, business meetings, picnics and other functions. Just one specialty off the catering menu is a wheel of creamy brie surrounded by a homemade crusty, cracked wheat braid.

Getting There

Head north on I-5 and take the Edmonds-Kingston ferry Exit. Continue west into downtown Edmonds on Fifth Avenue. brusseau's is on the corner of Fifth and Dayton, across from the Old Milltown.

Jerilyn is devoted to preparing fresh local foods in innovative ways.

HOME BY THE SEA

Address:	2388 East Sunlight Beach Road, Clinton, WA 98236
Telephone:	(206) 221-2964
Location:	On the southwest coast of Whidbey Island, six miles from the Clinton ferry
Hosts:	Sharon Fritts-Drew, Helen Fritts, Joyce Fritts Alexander
Room & Cottage Rates:	$55 - $110
Credit Cards:	MasterCard, Visa
Remarks:	No pets. Room rates include full breakfast; cottages provided with "Breakfast Baskets"and complete kitchen. Senior packages available.

Whidbey Island is the longest island in the contiguous United States, stretching north and south for nearly 50 miles in Washington's Puget Sound. On the southwest corner of the island, tucked under Double Bluff, is Useless Bay. Upon the shore of this wide, shallow bay is the Home by the Sea — Whidbey Island's first bed and breakfast.

Innkeeper Sharon Fritts-Drew has taught in several different countries and traveled in 43. She created the bed and breakfast on the beach where she returned every summer for 20 years; the place where she encourages others to "take a pause from the hurried world." Upon arrival at Home by the Sea, the aroma of candles and cookies permeates the air, and the pace of the city is soon shed. The Fritts-Drew family offers two rooms in the main house. Four additional cottages are located within a five-mile radius. The smorgasbord of choices include the Nordic Cottage on Lone Lake with private fishing dock; Cape Cod Cottage, a 1940s sea coast family accommodation with beach access; and Swiss Chalet and Chanterelle tucked in fir and pine trees for a totally relaxing experience.

At Home

Guest rooms in the Home face west for a view across the bay to the Olympic Mountains. A natural bird sanctuary, this sandy realm is home to eagles, geese, ducks and sandpipers. Both the "Sunset Room" and the "Seabreeze Suite" have double beds and private baths. The latter also offers a sitting room with a single bed. Sharon's multi-cultural accents — an Egyptian camel footstool, a Turkish brass urn, and a collection of beaded purses — grace each room. In the closets hang plush bathrobes for your excursion to the hot tub, which is on a deck near the beach.

The living room, with its broad picture windows facing the bay, is furnished with Persian rugs and Middle Eastern treasures. Breakfast is served in the neighboring dining room with the same spectacular view. Standard morning fare is eggs Benedict, crepes or soufflé, accompanied by homemade muffins and breads, juice, fresh fruit and brewed coffee or tea.

The separate Swiss Chalet sits alone in acres of trees.

Not Inn

Home by the Sea's four cottages offer the ultimate in atmosphere and seclusion. Each has a fully equipped kitchen stocked with a special "Breakfast Basket." Tables are pre-set with elegant china, and guests may rise at their leisure to prepare breakfast. Wood and kindling are provided for each place. The cottages have minimum stay requirements on the weekends, so it is best to check with Sharon when making reservations.

Just down the road from the Home, the 1940s Cape Cod Cottage serves as a perfect family retreat with two double beds, a child's single and a crib. The natural cedar interior is accented by a Kabul camel blanket, antique furniture and a brick fireplace. A picnic table and barbeque are found in the backyard, which overlooks Deer Lagoon.

The Nordic Cottage, three miles from the Fritts-Drew home, overlooks quiet Lone Lake. A private dock floats in the lily pads, and the lake is known for excellent trout fishing in summer and ice-skating in winter. Its wood-burning stove, Danish lace curtains, hardwood floors, and Norwegian treasures create a romantic getaway. The cozy bedroom features a double bed and a lake view. A large, open kitchen with butcher block counters and a dishwasher make food preparation easy.

Sequestered in a deep forest, just five miles from the Home by the Sea, are two charming cottages: the Swiss Chalet and the Chanterelle. The Hansel and Gretel style Swiss Chalet is decorated with floral print wallpaper and French lace. Upstairs, an Eiderdown covers each double bed. The beds are romantically located under a skylighted ceiling. Nearby, on the same two acres of fir and pine, is the Chanterelle Cottage. A brick planter and flower trellis brighten

The main house faces Useless Bay.

the outside with a glider swing in a forest setting. Lace pillow slips accent the cottage's double bed. Prints from Morrocco and Spain are displayed on the living room walls, and a wood burning stove warms the room.

Out and About

Nearby Merkerk Rhododendron Gardens is a special treat for flower lovers. From March through May, grand bushes reaching 25 feet in height display brilliant flowers of all shades. Coupeville, located mid-island on Penn Cove, is one of the oldest towns in the state. It features Victorian homes, an 1855 blockhouse, and specialty shops and restaurants. The alluring town of Langley is an artists' community, and its main street is lined with shops of Northwest arts, crafts and collectibles.

Whidbey is an island of pasture land, farms and barns. A drive along its winding roads will lead you through rural communities to the Greenbank Berry Farm, the largest loganberry field in the world. Tours are available, as well as a tasting room for Chateau Ste. Michelle wines.

Getting There

Home by the Sea is reached by driving north on I-5 from Seattle to the Mukilteo—Clinton ferry, Exit 189 (11 miles). Drive four miles to the ferry landing and board the Washington State ferry for a 15-minute ride. Drive on Highway 525 north for six miles to Bayview center. Turn left on Howard Road and left again on Bayview Road. Continue one mile to Sunlight Beach Road and turn right. Please be extra cautious when driving down this narrow beach road. There are often children at play. Continue to the end of the road; the inn is on the left.

TURTLEBACK FARM INN

Address: Route 1, P.O. Box 650, Eastsound, WA 98245
Telephone: (206) 376-4914
Location: Six miles from Orcas Island ferry landing
in Crow Valley
Hosts: Bill and Susan Fletcher, Innkeepers
Room Rates: $50 to $110.
Credit Cards: MasterCard, Visa
Remarks: No smoking inside, no pets

Turtleback Mountain swells up from the west lobe of Orcas Island, one of nearly 172 islands in Washington State's San Juan Archipelago. The island's rim is 125 miles of arythmic coastline. Its interior is a collage of valleys, ponds and meadows. Upon one of these meadows, submerged in tranquility, rests the Turtleback Farm Inn.

Complete Restoration

This restored 100-year-old farmhouse has all the charm of a country manor. The setting is serene, complete with grasslands, barns and outbuildings, 300-year-old maples and a pond well stocked with trout (catch and release). Turtleback Farm Inn, completely renovated by the Fletchers in 1985, combines country farmhouse living with a comfortable guest retreat.

Hanging on the wall inside the front door is an ad from the September 22, 1933, Seattle Daily Times, featuring the film *Tarzan the Fearless*. The ad reads, "Buster Crabbe, muscular Olympic swimming champion, whose latest screen appearance brings excitement aplenty to the Roxy Theater." The famous actor, who recently passed away, is Susan's father.

A Touch of Class

Each of Turtleback's seven individually decorated guest rooms reflect the Fletchers' careful attention to detail. All are unique, from the "Meadow Room" with its expansive view to the "Bunk Room," which is reminiscent of a ship's cabin. Spotless Northwest fir floors throughout the inn are softened by imported rugs. French floral print cottons envelope woolly comforters — some of the wool is directly from the backs of the sheep grazing outside. The living room is a cozy gathering place for inn guests.

Fresh Start

Dining room tables are set with stark white linens, fine china and silver, and a turtle-shaped trivet with a pot of freshly ground coffee or brewed tea. Fresh juice and fruits begin the meal. During the summer there are fresh berries from the island; the fall brings apples from the trees right on the farm. Next comes

The 100-year-old farmhouse overlooks 80 acres of the original homestead.

Susan's famed granola. (She'll proudly share the recipe.) As diners crunch along, Susan is busy preparing the next course, which may be an omelette served with muffins or homemade bread, or perhaps a corn waffle accompanied by sausage or bacon. Celtic harp music wafts in from the kitchen as guests begin their Orcas day in fine fashion.

An Orcas For Everyone

Trails descend from Turtleback Farm Inn into the meadows below. Domestic chickens, ducks and geese share the land with several varieties of migratory birds. Forests, pastures and meadows are yours to explore, with picnic spots and private places in every direction.

A visitor to Orcas will not leave Turtleback Inn without a map of the island, complete with Fletchers' heiroglyphics denoting points of interest, as well as some personal advise on what to see and do. As Bill says, "These are some of the richest waters I've seen." Fishing is always a favorite sport as Orcas' waters are an obliging host to salmon and cod. Bicycling, sailing, canoeing and kayaking are common island activities. A walk along the beach at Obstruction Pass is a prime way to view sea lions and perhaps the dorsal fin of an Orca whale disappearing into the sound—there are 88 resident Orcas who pass by regularly.

Cascade Lake at Moran State Park is a wonderful place to stretch out after a long sleep at Turtleback. In addition to swimming, the lake offers bass and trout fishing from small rental boats, or a chance to try out the paddle boats.

Hikers will enjoy circumnavigating Cascade Lake, or one of the many other trails in Moran State Park. An easy quarter-mile walk through the forest brings

Many of the spacious rooms have a private balcony.

hikers to Rustic and Cascade Falls. For the more ambitious, Mt. Constitution awaits — its 2,400 feet creates a challenging hike to the highest point in the San Juan archipelago, but the view is well worth the effort.

Off-Season Orcas

Midweek and off-season visitors will be rewarded with the added serenity and true flavor of the island. Crowds are down, the pace is slower, so there is simply more of the island's charm just for you. Fall colors brighten the landscape, and spring brings the pastels of flowering plants and trees. Winter comes with its own mood, complete with storms and misty nights.

Returning to the Turtleback Farm Inn's welcoming fire is a fine way to end the day. Guests are invited to use the wet bar, which is always stocked with special teas, coffees and cocoa. There is also a decanter of sherry on a nearby cart.

Bill and Susan live in a separate home on the farm, so in the evening when they retire to their home, guests can experience having the entire farmhouse to themselves. This is an ideal situation if you come up with your own group during the off-season and occupy the entire inn.

Getting There

Orcas Island may be reached by Lake Union Air or via the Washington state ferry from Anacortes. From Seattle take I-5 north and follow the signs to the Anacortes ferry landing. Upon arrival on Orcas, drive two and one-half miles on Horseshoe Highway. Turn left at the road sign which indicates Turtleback Farm Inn. Travel one mile and turn right on Crow Valley. Continue 2.4 miles to the inn.

CHRISTINA'S

Address:	Main Street, Eastsound, WA 98245
Telephone:	(206) 376-4904
Location:	On Main Street in Eastsound, Orcas Island
Host:	Christina Gentry
Cuisine:	Natural Northwest
Prices:	$12.50 TO $17.50
Credit Cards:	American Express, Carte Blanche, Diner's Club, MasterCard, Visa
Hours:	6 p.m. to midnight daily June 12 to August 15. 5 p.m. to 10 p.m. Thursday through Monday the rest of the year. Brunch served Sunday from 9:30 a.m. Closed New Year's Day to Valentine's Day.

This little hamlet on the shore of Orcas Island's Eastsound Bay seems an unlikely spot for one of the state's top-rated restaurants. Eastsound's Main Street runs little more than four blocks and houses only a singlestructure taller than one story. That building is the Island Union Building, and its second story contains Christina's, a cozy restaurant with a broad view of the shoreline and the bay.

Orcas Island is but one in the chain of 172 San Juan islands. One of the largest islands, it sports a year-round population of nearly 1,500. Visitors enjoy the diversity of scenery and activities on Orcas, from the 2,409-foot Mt. Constitution to the secluded beaches rimming the island. Eastsound is the hub of culture and cuisine. Both visitors and locals alike recognize Christina's as "the" restaurant on the island.

Natural Northwest Cuisine

Christina Gentry selects and prepares the meals herself. Fresh, locally grown products include seafood from the cold waters of Puget Sound, oysters from the island, mussels from nearby Lopez Island, poultry and lamb from Lopez and Orcas islands, and produce from local farms.

All meals are prepared with simplicity and distinction. Few sauces, if any, are used in most dishes, reflecting Christina's stong belief that the natural flavors of the food should remain pure. "This is what I call natural Northwest cooking," she says. "I want to serve only fresh local products as simply and purely as is possible." For instance, the restaurant's generous serving of poached salmon is glazed with basil, then served with a fresh garden salad, fresh vegetables and just-picked new potatoes.

The menus change with the season and the readiness of the natural ingredients. The poultry may be pheasant, game hen or chicken. The meat may be a different cut each evening. A specialty is the rich Christina's bouillabaisse, lavishly packed with fresh, local shellfish and served with one of the 50 or 60 regional wines stocked by Christina.

Desserts Worth Waiting For

Christina's desserts bring back the meaning to after-dinner treats. She serves fresh berry tarts, or homemade ice cream, such as lavender honey and espresso, homemade piña colada cheesecake, or her legendary chocolate mousse tart.

A Homey Setting

A former art student, Christina takes pride in her collection of Oriental rugs, copperware and old kitchen implements almost as much as her culinary skills. "I guess that I just transferred my artistic bent from art to cooking," she says.

The restaurant is a blend of both talents. Each table has a direct view of the bay; the blue tablecloths capture and extend the colors of the sea. Fresh flowers and chic china add elegance to the setting. Oil lamps provide soft light, blending with the setting sun.

There is a marvelous postage-stamp-size lounge off of the dining room for dining, or relaxing over a drink before or after the meal. The room is so small that there are only three stools at the bar and five tables that seat two, but it's cozy and personable, and they serve generous cocktails.

Getting There

In Eastsound, the two-story Island Union Building on Main Street is easily recognizable; turn into the adjacent alley and walk up the stairs.

Twilight is a favorite time here.

HIGH COUNTRY PACKERS

Address: P.O. Box 108, Issaquah, WA 98027
Telephone: (206) 392-0111
Location: Thirty miles outside Cle Elum up the North Fork of the
                 Teanaway River
Hosts: Robert C. Folkman, Outfitter and Chief Guide, and
                 Debbie Gallie, Camp Director and Head Cook
Rates: From $75 per person for guided day
                 ($40 for one-half day) to $110 per person per day
                 for extended pack trips
Remarks: Reservations required. Credit cards not accepted.
                 Summer youth camps through Labor Day. Special
                 fishing and hunting camps also available.

High Country Packers, an experienced outfitting service operating in the Wenatchee National Forest and Alpine Lakes Wilderness, offers hikers the chance to enjoy the invigorating sights, sounds and smells of the back country for a day or two or a week. There's something purifying about the whole experience, whether it's riding a mountain-wise quarterhorse into deep and wild country, or gathering around a friendly campfire on the edge of an alpine meadow as the moon eases over the rim of a sentinel peak.

High Country Packers takes away the strains of traditional wilderness hiking. The guides and wranglers are proficient horsemen and experts in outdoor living. Led by Bob Folkman, an affable and competent guide, the wranglers carefully match horses and riders before setting out. The trail-wise animals are manageable even for the most inexperienced rider. All the gear and food for your trip is carried by dependable mules. It doesn't take long before everyone settles into the rhythm of the trail and begins to enjoy the surroundings.

Routes Aplenty

Depending on the length of your trip, you might venture up the DeRoux trail and pass the Elsinore mine and smelter, from which mercury and gold were taken early in this century. Or you may head directly into the Alpine Lakes Wilderness and follow the Hardscrabble/Turnpike route into Ingals Lake where mountain goat and elk are often spotted. Atop a saddle ridge between Esmeralda Basin and VanEpps Pass, at an elevation of over 7,000 feet, you will be treated to a spectacular view of the entire Cascade range, including Mount Rainier, Mount Baker and Glacier Peak. Other routes lead to high camps such as Berry Basin, Skookum and Jolly Basin, each of which is situated in an alpine meadow encircled by craggy ridges. At any one of these pristine spots you might spot deer, elk or bear.

Half-day tours leave the base camp and travel to Iron Peak. High Country Packers provides all the gear; all you need is warm clothing for those chilly mountain nights, a good sleeping bag and your personal items.

In Camp

The trek is only half the fun of a High Country vacation. At the end of each day's ride, you make camp. You can either pitch in and help or sit back and let Bob and his crew do the work. Debbie Gallie, head cook and camp director, is famous for her dutch-oven pioneer meals. The oven is placed next to the open fire and hot embers are laid on the lid to cook the food. There might be a hearty beef stew or chicken in that deep pot, but, whatever it is on the menu, there will be more than enough. You can also look forward to sourdough bread and a freshly baked dessert to round off the meal.

Evenings in camp are communal times to unwind, tell stories, watch the fire and gaze at the bright stars. A sound sleep is assured in the comfortable, domed tents. Come morning you awaken to the gurgling sound of coffee brewing on the open fire and the restless stirring of the horses. There's freshly baked coffeecake and biscuits to go with a sausage omelette. One last cup of cowboy coffee and you're back in the saddle again. High Country also operates an excellent camp for children. Call Debbie for details.

Getting There

From Seattle, take I-90 east past Cle Elum to Exit 85. Continue toward Wenatchee on State Route 970 for seven miles. Turn left on Teanaway Road and follow the North Fork of the Teanaway River 13 miles to the end of the pavement. Bear right and follow the dirt road for eight miles, turning left at the Stafford Creek and Beverly Creek junctions. The High Country Packers/Camp Wahoo sign will be on the left.

Discover the fun of exploring on horseback.

Vancouver

British Columbia

In our travels throughout British Columbia, Mardi and I have been struck by its raw, muscular beauty. It spans over ten percent of Canada and covers 365,960 square miles. Its population centers heavily around a few urban areas, Victoria and Vancouver, leaving the rest of the province sparsely developed and scenically spectacular. From the jagged fjord-carved coast of Vancouver Island to the long, glittering inland lakes, we've seen diverse and unparalleled beauty. Mystical islands, ice-chiseled mountain ranges, tropical hot springs and rolling range lands are all a part of this province's mosaic.

British Columbia's nine thousand years of native cultural history is as fascinating as its physical setting is dramatic. Intrepid coastal peoples, the Haida, Kwakiutl, Nootka, Taglish, Tlingit, Tsimshian and Wakashan, congregated where fish were plentiful. Inland tribes, the Salish and Kootenays, were generally nomadic and depended on hunting for survival. Today, these people are famous for their high quality crafts, masks and totem poles, weavings and ceremonial regalia — all testimony to a skilled and highly developed ancestry. Ancient petroglyphs, or rock carvings, are among the cultural legacies left by these peoples. Mardi and I love to walk the beach on Quadra Island where over 50 petroglyphs remain intact. The days of potlatches, tribal wars and cedar longhouses are all a part of B.C.'s cultural fabric, as are the myths, legends and beliefs of the native Canadians. Descendants of the tribal people strive to preserve their heritage in the ever-changing world. The most comprehensive collection of artifacts to be found is in Victoria's Provincial Museum. We've spent entire afternoons wandering among the displays, sensing the strength and character exhibited by the work of these people.

British Columbia is also a part of the Pacific Rim. The culture is rich with people from an increasing number of countries including India, Vietnam, Thailand, Malaysia, China and Japan. Their distinct influences are evident in the arts and cuisine, particularly in the larger cities. Large groups of Chinese laborers came to work on the construction of the cross-Canada railroad in the late 19th century. Vancouver and Victoria both have famous Chinatowns begun by these early pioneers.

Today's largest group of inhabitants are the descendants of English, Scottish, Irish and Welsh immigrants. Canadians are warm and hospitable people, perhaps more polite and conversive than Americans. A close community spirit prevails even in the larger cities, making travel easy and enjoyable. We recall many pleasureable evenings spent around tables loaded with British Columbia bounties, swapping stories and sharing a glass of wine with our Canadian friends and neighbors.

Travel Tips for British Columbia

Canada operates on the metric system, which often causes the average U.S. citizen to stop and ponder the conversions. A few simple and east to remember guidelines are as follows:

Distances and speed limits are posted in kilometers. To convert kilometers to miles, drop the last digit and multiply by six. To convert miles to kilometers, multiply by 1.6. Thus, 100 km/hr = 10 x 6 = 60 mi/hr.

Gasoline is measured in liters. One liter equals .26 gallons, one gallon equals 3.79 liters.

Temperatures are measured on the Celsius scale. To convert Celsius to Fahrenheit, multiply by nine-fifths and add 32. To convert from Fahrenheit to Celsius, subtract 32 and multiply by five-ninths.

British Columbia requires visiting motorists to produce evidence of financial responsibility if involved in an accident. The use of seat belts is compulsory.

Visitors are urged to exchange currency soon after arrival into British Columbia. Normal banking hours are 10 a.m. to 3 p.m. Monday through Friday. Trust companies, credit unions, cooperatives, and caisse populaire are also able to exchange U.S. dollars for Canadian dollars. Most shops and businesses will accept U.S. dollars, but will most likely offer a lower exchange rate. At the time of this writing, one U.S. dollar is worth about one-third more than one Canadian dollar.

Major American bank and credit cards are honored in Canada. Purchases are billed at the U.S. dollar equivalent of the Canadian price. British Columbia's retail sales tax is seven percent on most purchases. The exceptions are: clothing for children under 15, books, patent medicines, yard goods. Hotel rooms, campgrounds, liquor and meals are all subject to the tax.

Transportation

British Columbia is served by airlines providing local, trans-continental, and international service through Vancouver and Victoria International Airports. Bus lines and a passenger rail connect B.C. with the United States and the rest of Canada. The province has over 8,000 miles of paved highways. But, one of the most scenic and unique modes of travel in British Columbia is the B.C. Ferry System. With its more than 25 ships and web of routes, it is one of the largest and most efficient in the world. For many, a ferry ride is one of the most memorable parts of their visit.

Three-hundred-mile-long Vancouver Island, traversed by a modern highway stretching along its eastern edge, is also accessible by a number of ferry routes. B.C. Ferries operates two routes between the Greater Vancouver area and Vancouver Island: Tsawwassen to Swartz Bay (one hour and 35 minutes) and Horseshoe Bay to Nanaimo (one hour and 30 minutes). Departures on both routes run nearly hourly during the summer, but less frequently during winter. The same ferry system takes you to Salt Spring and the other Gulf Islands. Tsawwassen to Salt Spring Island is a two and three-quarter hour crossing, while Swartz Bay to Salt Spring Island takes about one-half hour. Another Vancouver Island departure is from Crofton to Salt Spring Island, which takes only 20 minutes. Recorded information for B.C. ferries is available in Victoria by calling (604) 656-0757. In Vancouver, call (604) 669-1121; in Nanaimo call (604) 753-6626.

The Washington State Ferry System operates between Anacortes, Washington and Sidney B.C. The crossing takes about three hours and operates twice daily in summer, once daily in winter. Summer vehicle reservations are recommended. For schedules, call: Victoria (604) 656-1531 or 381-1551; Seattle (206) 464-6400.

Blackball Transport operates the M.V. Coho between Port Angeles, on Washington's Olympic Peninsula, and Victoria, with multiple daily sailings. In Victoria, call (604) 386-2202 for information and schedules; in Port Angeles, call (206) 457-4491.

The water jet catamaran Victoria Clipper offers a two and one-half hour cruise from Seattle to Victoria for walk-on passengers only. Year-round daily service. Seattle (206) 448-5000, Victoria (604) 382-8100.

Customs and Border Crossings

All visitors must clear Canadian customs when entering B.C. and when returning to the United States. It is a simple procedure, yet there are a few regulations. Border traffic tends to be heavier on weekends, particularly Sunday nights, so plan accordingly. Passports are not necessary for U.S. citizens; however, proof of citizenship is required. If you are bringing dogs or cats over three months old, you must have a certificate of rabies vaccination within the past 36 months. Canadian customs regulations permit you to bring personal baggage, recreational equipment, two days' food supply and your vehicle. All non-consumable items must leave the country with you.

When reentering the United States, you may bring back $400 (U.S. dollars) worth of duty-free articles for personal or household use or as gifts, if you have been out of the country for at least 48 hours. Additionally, you must not have claimed the exemption in the past 30 days. You may include for exemption 100 cigars and 200 cigarettes, and one liter of wine, beer or liquor. Your exemption is $25 (U.S. dollars) if you have been gone less than 48 hours or have claimed the $400 exemption within the past 30 days. You may include 50 cigarettes, 10 cigars, five ounces of alcoholic beverages, and five ounces of perfume containing alcohol or proportionate amounts of each. When entering the U.S., you must declare, at the price paid, everything acquired in Canada that you are taking home, including gifts given to you and articles worn or used. Articles imported in excess of your exemption will be subject to duty. Penalties apply for failure to declare. Direct specific customs inquiries to: Revenue Customs, Customs and Excise, Public Relations Branch, Ottawa, Ontario, Canada, K1A 0L5 (613) 993-6220.

Shopping in British Columbia

British Columbia's myriad influences and cultures, from English to native, have created an unique array of products for purchase. Furs and Hudson's Bay blankets, Irish linens and lace, old-fashioned quilts and pewter are traditionally good buys. Imported china and crystal are in abundance in the major cities. British Columbia jade is considered among the world's finest. Bulky woolen Cowichan sweaters and fur-trimmed Inuit parkas, as well as wood carvings, original prints and bead and quill works, are among the native crafts. Be certain to save all receipts from purchase for customs declaration.

Liquor Laws

The minimum drinking age in British Columbia is 19. All alcoholic beverages by the bottle (including wine and beer) are sold in provincial liquor stores. In smaller communities, retail stores are licensed to sell alcohol and are generally open Monday through Saturday until about 6 p.m. (Closed Sundays and holidays.) Penalties are stiff for drinking and driving, and are strictly enforced. It is a criminal offense for a driver to refuse to provide a breath or blood sample when required by a Peace Officer.

Weather

Coastal British Columbia is typically cool and wet during the fall, winter and spring, with mild, sunny summers. Victoria may often be warmer than Vancouver as it lies in the rain shadow of the Olympic Mountains. Temperatures in both cities average daytime highs of 71°F and nighttime lows of 55°F in August. In October the highs average around 56°F and the lows around 34°F. July is the sunniest month; December the rainiest.

Fishing and Hunting Regulations

Licenses are required for fresh and saltwater fishing. Information regarding fresh water fishing and hunting licenses may be obtained from:

Ministry of the Environment
Parliament Building
Victoria, British Columbia
Canada V8V 1X4

Information on saltwater licenses may be obtained from:

Department of Fisheries and Oceans
1090 West Pender Street
Vancouver, B.C. Canada V6E 2P1

Information Sources for British Columbia

British Columbia's Travel InfoCentre Network is designed to assist travelers with most travel needs. InfoCentre signs are prominently displayed on highways and in towns, and B.C. has over 140 offices in the system. For information, contact:
Minister of Tourism, Recreation and Culture
Parliament Buildings
Victoria, B.C. Canada V8V 1X4
(604) 387-1642

In Seattle:
720 Olive Way
Seattle, WA 98101
(206) 623-5937

Selected British Columbia Events

January
Steelhead Fishing — April Point Lodge
Winter Carnival — Courtenay

February
Chinese New Year Celebration — Vancouver
Annual Flower Count — Victoria

March
Kandahar Ski Races — Courtenay

April
"Terrifvic" Victoria Jazz Party — Victoria
Salmon Fishing Starts at April Point — Quadra Island

May
Festival of Murals — Chemainus
Swiftsure Boat Races — Victoria
Vancouver Marathon — Vancouver

June
Fly Fishing School — Hatheume Lake Resort
Sea Capers Weekend — Salt Spring Island

July
Campbell River Salmon Festival — Campbell River
All Sooke Days — Sooke
World Championship Bathtub Races — Nanaimo

August
Comox Airshow — Comox
Salmon Festival — Port Alberni
Air Show — Abbotsford

September
Pacific National Exhibition — Vancouver
Classic Boat Festival — Victoria
Island Arts and Crafts Fair — Ganges / Salt Spring Island

October
Wine Festival — Okanagan
October Fest — Campbell River
Children's Festival Day — Victoria

November
Remembrance Day — All Communities

December
Santa Claus Parade — Victoria

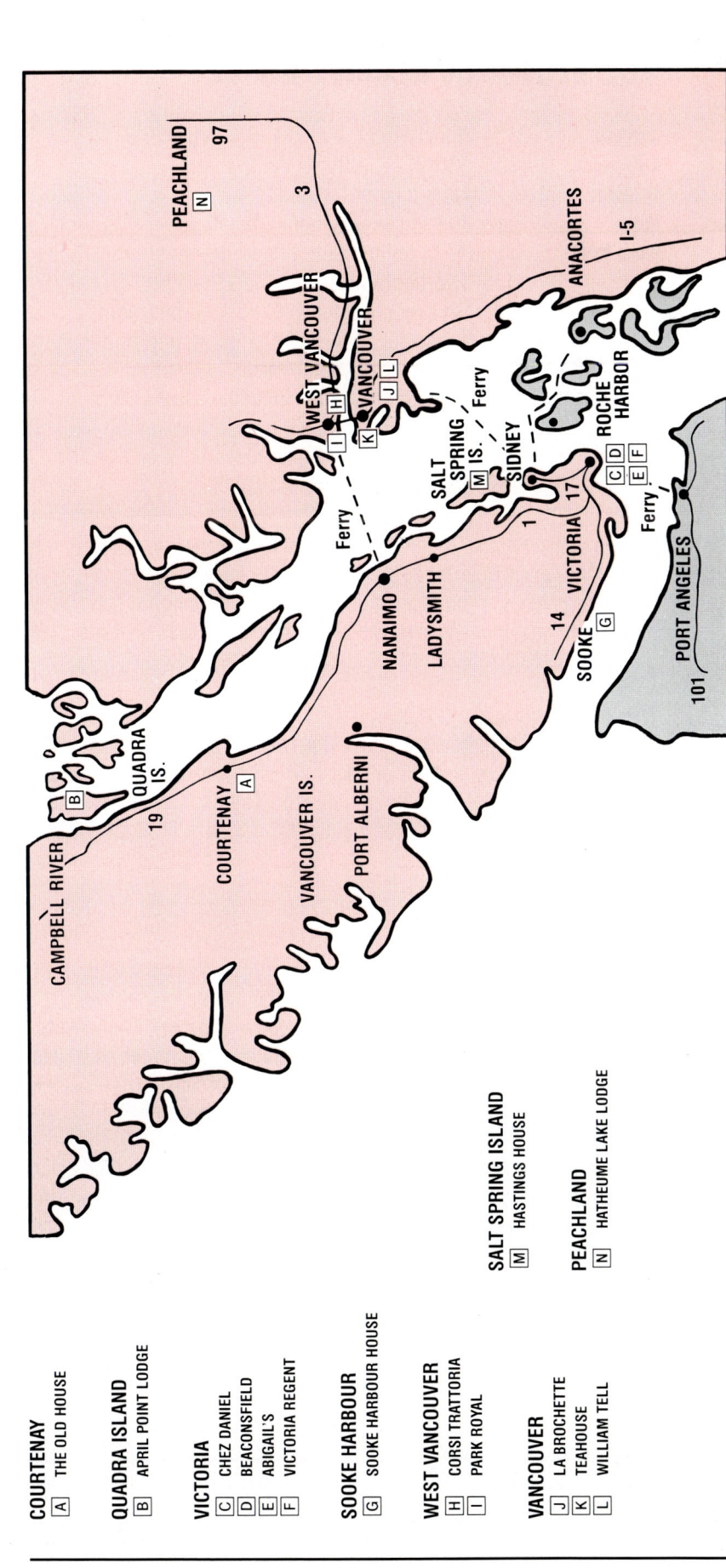

COURTENAY
A THE OLD HOUSE

QUADRA ISLAND
B APRIL POINT LODGE

VICTORIA
C CHEZ DANIEL
D BEACONSFIELD
E ABIGAIL'S
F VICTORIA REGENT

SOOKE HARBOUR
G SOOKE HARBOUR HOUSE

WEST VANCOUVER
H CORSI TRATTORIA
I PARK ROYAL

VANCOUVER
J LA BROCHETTE
K TEAHOUSE
L WILLIAM TELL

SALT SPRING ISLAND
M HASTINGS HOUSE

PEACHLAND
N HATHEUME LAKE LODGE

THE VICTORIA REGENT HOTEL

Address: 1234 Wharf Street, Victoria, B.C. V8W 3H9
Telephone: (604) 386-2211; (800) 663-7472
Location: On Victoria's Inner Harbour
Host: Peter Bueschkens, General Manager
Room Rates: Single $75, double $85, one-bedroom suites $115 to $145, two-bedroom suites $170 to $190. One-bedroom Executive suites $220; two-bedroom Executive suites $250 to $270, three-bedroom suites $495 (Canadian). Additional person $15.
Credit Cards: American Express, Carte Blanche, Diners Club, MasterCard, Visa
Remarks: Children under 16 (with parents) free of charge. No pets. Non-smoking rooms available.

Victoria's Inner Harbour is one of the loveliest parts of the city, and staying at the Victoria Regent Hotel is one of the best ways to enjoy it. The upscale, eight story hotel perches on the edge of the Inner Harbour, offering a stunning view of the entire waterfront. Visiting yachts moor along the seawall; landscaped grounds and the ornate Parliament buildings rim the harbor.

Watch passenger boats slide gracefully into their slips, sailboats venture off to sea, fleets of fishing boats return with their bounty, and float planes land in the harbour and tie up at the hotel's dock. The Parliament buildings, edged by over 4,000 tiny white lights at night, shine brilliantly against the sky. These and other sights are viewed from the comfort of your suite at the Victoria Regent.

Victoria's Best Kept Secret

The Victoria Regent has been referred to as "Victoria's best kept secret," offering a selection of accommodations that are both affordable and luxurious, and a courteous staff who is willing to assist guest in any way. Upon arrival, guests descend garden steps, traversing vibrantly-hued flower beds, and enter the lobby where the immediate sensation is that of comfort. The Victoria Regent is a fine blend of hotel hospitality and at-home warmth.

Accommodations are in individual rooms or very spacious suites. The suites are so spacious, some upwards of 1,000 square feet, that guests say they return for that reason. But, there are plenty of other reasons to enjoy the Victoria Regent.

The hotel's suites offer a unique floor plan to take advantage of the supreme views. Many have a balcony overlooking the waterfront, while others offer expansive city-scapes. The apartment style suites are fully carpeted and appointed in tasteful contemporary decor. A fully equipped kitchen, up to two bedrooms, a dining area and living room comprise the accommodations. Executive suites also have a fireplace, den and jacuzzi. Queen and king sized beds are used throughout. Each two-bedroom suite offers two full bathrooms.

Beautiful views of the Inner Harbour Cove come with the rooms.

The Victoria Regent offers all the amenities you would expect from a fine hotel. A courtesy limousine is available to meet guests at the Victoria Clipper or other arrival points in Victoria. It may also be utilized for limited service in the downtown area. Babysitting services may be arranged, laundry facilities are open for guests' use. Complimentary morning newspaper is delivered to the room and complimentary satellite television is standard in all rooms.

The Victoria Regent offers café and room service with full English or Continental breakfast. Homemade soups, fresh salads and deli sandwiches are on the lunch menu, as well as a limited selection of hot items. Dinners catered to the suites may be arranged for private parties and corporate gatherings, or for an intimate evening on your private balcony. A favorite is to have the catered dinner on the balcony at sunset. The meal can be made even more complete with personalized table service.

Central Location

The hotel's convenient location lends itself to exploring Victoria on foot. Complimentary security underground parking is available to guests, so it's easy to leave the car behind. A full-time concierge is located in the hotel's lobby to assist guests in travel plans and local information.

Most of Victoria's shopping and sightseeing is located within a few blocks of the hotel Nearby Bastions Square, running between Wharf and Government Streets, is lined with shops, restaurants and art galleries. Government Street, too, is considered one of Victoria's prime shopping streets. Victoria's Information Centre is located on Government Street, and is another valuable source of information for sightseeing and dining.

Catered meals are available on your private balcony.

Gone Fishing

The Victoria Regent offers fishing charters that depart from its marina and may be arranged for any desired length of time. Expert guides are on hand to point out prime fishing locations near Victoria, where Coho and Chinook salmon are among the catches. Sailboats, too, may be chartered for a day trip into the local waters. Marina facilities are available to those arriving by boat, and the dock is conveniently located for seaplane arrivals and departures.

Parks, Gardens and Museums

A walk or drive through the quaint streets of Victoria will immediately pull your attention to her ultra-green lawns and well-tended flower beds. Double-decker London buses depart from near the Victoria Regent for tours.

The rococo Parliament buildings are a palace-like stone structure surrounded by nearly 13 acres of grounds that house the seat of the government for the province. Visitors may take guided tours and hear debates when the house is in session. Mosaic tiles, intricate stained glass windows and Italian marble are part of the decor in these late 1800's buildings. Outside features of the Parliament building include well tended gardens bordering finely kept lawns, the Centennial Fountain, which commemorates the founding of the Colony of British Columbia in 1858, and a collection of statues portraying Queen Victoria and numerous writers, philosophers and pioneers.

Getting There

To reach the Victoria Regent, follow Government Street north past the yacht basin. Turn left onto Wharf Street and continue two blocks to the hotel.

BEACONSFIELD INN

Address:	998 Humboldt Street, Victoria, B.C. V8V 2Z8
Telephone:	(604) 384-4044
Location:	A few blocks from downtown Victoria
Host:	Sydney Varley, Innkeeper
Room Rates:	$75 - $155 (CDN) $55 to $115 (U.S.) two persons.
Credit Cards:	MasterCard, Visa
Remarks:	No pets. Rates include breakfast.

The first thing you notice as you mount the steps to the stately Beaconsfield Inn is the sign which reads "City of Victoria Heritage Building." Next, as you pass through double doors etched with a grand peacock, you enter a black-and-white tiled sun room appointed with wicker furniture, stained glass, and huge potted plants. Passing through another set of doors, you are suddenly in an entryway of high ceilings, dark polished mahogany floors, antique stuffed birds and massive furniture. It is a step into another world — the Edwardian Period, "the height of the British Empire," during which clean, balanced lines created an elegant simplicity.

A Wedding Gift

Beaconsfield Inn was built by millionaire R.P. Rithet in 1905 as a wedding gift for his only daughter. The Edwardian mansion has been restored to its former elegance and carefully designed to portray the feeling of the era. Its decor reflects the tastes of the wealthy class who were reacting against the busy frivolity of the Victorian period.

Situated on a corner in a residential area near the heart of Victoria, Beaconsfield was at one time a nursing home. Purchased in 1973 by Bill McKechnie, it underwent serious renovation to return the building to its original design. The architectural drawings were retrieved from the University of Victoria's archives, and Bill scoured antique auctions for the ideal mix of furnishings in keeping with the design.

Edwardian Mansion

Each of the inn's 12 guest rooms is decorated to retain the design of a "typical" Edwardian mansion. A few of the rooms are named for individuals who were prominent during the period. For instance, there is an Oscar Wilde room and Lilly Langtree (King Edward VII's mistress) room. Lillie's Room features a canopied bed, fireplace and heated towel racks.

Other names reflect the tone or feature of the room, such as the Rosebud Room, painted with pale rose and cream hues; the Blue Room, most definitely blue, with an alcove; or the Verandah Room, with its vintage wicker parlor

The inn is situated in a quiet neighborhood just blocks from the Inner Harbour.

furniture. All rooms have an elaborate private bath, down comforter and extended double or queen-size bed. The largest room, the Attic Suite, has a wet bar, private jacuzzi , fireplace and canopy bed. The Garden Suite, located on street level, opens onto an enclosed manicured garden, as does the smaller Gatekeeper Room. The smallest room is Willy's Room, which is cozy, but well suited to budget travel. Special touches add a personal note. Concierge service, fresh flowers, and an evening hot water bottle on a wintery eve. For honeymooners, there is a complimentary bottle of champagne.

The library is lined with leather furniture and extensive volumes of literature. Polished dark wood beams enhance the illusion that you have stepped into another era. An evening sherry hour in the library provides a chance to meet other guests. An inlaid wood table is the place for backgammon or chess.

Breakfast — coffee and juice, home baked goods and a daily entrée — is taken in the bright kitchen, served family style around an oak table. Eggs Beaconsfield, the cook's version of eggs Benedict, is a popular dish. Another favorite is salmon quiche.

As guests linger over fresh, hot coffee, they are apt to share travel tales and tips. Beaconsfield lends itself to this kind of relaxation and comraderie. Guests have a tendency to return to Beaconsfield again and again; the cards and letters displayed in the lobby give witness to their praise: "Absolutely fabulous. Great room, super breakfast. Marvelous."

Outside the Inn

Beaconsfield's location is ideal for seeing Victoria, and the innkeeper will gladly direct you. The British Columbia Provincial Museum is not far away.

The evening sherry hour takes place in the richly furnished library.

This world famous museum explores 12,000 years of natural and cultural history. A highlight features a recreation of a pioneer town, a coal mine shaft, a fish cannery, and Captain Cook's private cabin aboard his ship the *Discovery*. The newest exhibit features The Mysterious World of the Open Ocean. Explore the rich Indian cultural heritage of the Province's First Peoples in a stunning display of totem poles, masks and a Kwakuitl bighouse.

Victoria is a walking town, so simply taking a walk through one of the many parks is sure to liven your spirits. A lookout station at Beacon Hill Park, 184 acres of windswept knolls and colorful flower gardens, promises views of the ocean and mountains.

Golf is a year-round sport in Victoria at Glen Meadows Golf and Country Club on McTavish Road. At 6,800 yards, it is one of the longest courses in British Columbia. The Victoria Golf Club's spectacular 18-hole course overlooks the Strait of Juan de Fuca.

Drive along Beach Drive for another view of the Strait, and continue through Oak Bay to see the most handsome residential areas in the city. For a longer trip, drive north on Douglas Street through Goldstream Park to Malahat Drive. This route provides outstanding views of Mill Bay, Cowichan Bay, and the Gulf Islands in the distance.

Getting There

Follow Government Street along the inner harbor. Just past the Empress Hotel, turn right onto Humboldt Street. Cross Douglas, veering right. Continue for four blocks. The inn will be on a corner to your left.

ABIGAIL'S HOTEL

Address:	906 McClure Street, Victoria, B.C. V8V 3E7
Telephone:	(604) 388-5363
Location:	A few blocks from the heart of Victoria
Host:	Catherine Challinor, Innkeeper
Room Rates:	$75 to $155 (Canadian), double occupancy.
	Additional person $22 (Canadian)
	$55 to $115 (U.S.)
Credit Cards:	MasterCard, Visa
Remarks:	No pets. Rates include breakfast

"My guideline for the design of Abigail's was 'timeless,'" says owner Bill McKechnie."I kept thinking 'fanciful,' 'feminine' and 'timeless.'" Abigail's Hotel is a romantic inn set near Victoria's center. Rebuilt from a Tudor apartment building in 1985, it is reminiscent of a European style hotel. Vibrant pansies in carefully aligned beds and forest green and burnt orange trim set against a stucco exterior create a collage of appealing colors and textures. A copy of a Rodin sculpture of a young woman wearing a straw hat festooned with flowers rests on a table inside the front door. "This sculpture," Bill says, "was the influence for Abigail's theme."

Unique Perspective

Abigail's interior is a geometric masterpiece. Angled archways and vaulted ceilings create unique perspectives on the traditional Tudor design. Surprise nooks, notches and crannies add a humorous touch and evoke a childlike sense of discovery. Soft peach, rose, teal and ivory tones are used throughout the inn, tastefully woven into a homey quilt of color.

Abigail's hotel is set on a quiet residential cul-de-sac. Its four stories offer a broad selection of secluded rooms. Of the 16 rooms, ten feature fireplaces. In two of these, the fireplace is glass enclosed and adjoins the bathroom and living area. Guests may recline in the jacuzzi while viewing the fire. Abigail's service-minded staff keeps rooms stocked with wood so that even third floor residents can easily light a fire on chilly evenings.

Eight guest rooms offer these private bubbling baths, complete with water-proof pillows for total relaxation. The spacious tiled bathrooms are appointed with pedestal sinks and brass fixtures. Glittering crystal chandeliers, eyelet curtains and antiques grace each room. Goose down comforters accent the comfortable beds, four of which are canopied. Four rooms have refrigerators, and several feature pass-throughs by which breakfast may be discreetly delivered without disrupting guests' privacy. There are no televisions or telephones in the rooms. However, a pay phone is located by the front desk for guests' use.

The hotel is located in a quiet residential area just a few blocks from the busy downtown.

The library is the primary gathering place for the inn's guests. Stately burgundy couches center around the fireplace. The walls are lined with leather bound volumes. A social hour with wine and imported cheeses takes place in this room on weekends; it is the ideal spot for receptions and weddings.
A cheery breakfast room shares the main floor with the library. Light oak tables, a brick fireplace, and lace curtains create a welcoming atmosphere. Coffee is available starting at 7:30 a.m.; breakfast is served from 8 to 9:30 a.m.

The inn's cook, Ginnie, prepares a delightful meal from the open kitchen, and peers over the counter to chat with guests. Her farm on Cortes Island produces most of the fruit used in the inn's homemade jams. For starters, freshly baked muffins or coffeecake wait in baskets on the table. Next, guests feast on one of Ginnie's specials: eggs Florentine, baked eggs with smoked salmon and a paragus, or seasonal omelettes. Ginnie, who is used to cooking for a large fa.nily, believes in using only the freshest ingredients.

A picnic hamper may be ordered for lunch. A wicker basket lunch may included paté, cheese, fresh bread, cookies, fruit and wine or juice. Baskets should be ordered the night before.

In the Heart of Victoria

Abigail's location is ideal for exploring Victoria on foot. Just three blocks to the north, on Fort Street, there is a broad assortment of antique shops, for which Victoria is known. Auctions take place Tuesday and Friday evenings, and are likely to produce a real find for the collector.

Stroll along Government Street near the Inner Harbour for a look at many of Victoria's shops. Munro's Books, one of Canada's largest independent

The Canterbury Bell bathroom combines old and new with antiques and a modern jacuzzi.

bookstores, displays its many volumes in a restored historic building. Straith's, also on Government Street, is noted for its fine tailored clothing. Irish linens, tartans and native British Columbian art are among the many other shopping treasures.

A short drive from Abigails, on Rockland Street, is the Lt. Governor's Mansion. The well-maintained grounds are open to the public. Visit the Art Gallery of Greater Victoria, 1040 Moss Street, featuring one of the finest Japanese art collections in Canada. Nearby is the Craigcarroch Castle, built in 1851 by Robert Dunsmuir for his wife. It features 36 rooms and leaded glass windows imported from Italy.

The Emily Carr Gallery, in the 106-year-old Rithet Building at 1107 Wharf Street, pays tribute to the world renowned Victoria artist. A film introduces the "Laughing One's" life and work. The artist's original work and manuscripts, her colorful impressions of the sea, mountains and village scenes of the West Coast Indians are displayed.

For a visit to a neighborhood pub, try Spinnakers located on Lime Bay at the foot of Catherine Street. The pub is known for its home brewed ales and stouts. Hearty pub fare completes the old English spirit. Abigail's staff can provide maps for attractions throughout the southern end of the island.

Getting There

From the inner harbor head north on Government Street. Take an immediate right onto Humboldt Street. Continue four blocks to Vancouver Street. Turn left onto Vancouver and continue four and one-half blocks to McClure. Turn left. Abigail's is at the end of the cul-de-sac.

CHEZ DANIEL

Address: 2522 Estevan Avenue, Victoria, B.C. V8R2S7
Telephone: (604) 592-7424
Host: Daniel Rigollet, Owner, Chef de Cuisine.
Cuisine: Classic French with Nouvelle Cuisine
Prices: Entrees $10 to $34 entrees (Canadian)
Credit Cards: MasterCard, Visa
Hours: 5:30 to 10 p.m. Tuesday through Saturday. Closed Sunday, Monday and Canadian holidays.

The inauspicious exterior of Chez Daniel may be somewhat misleading. Tucked in a small group of up-scale shops on a quiet street of northeast Victoria, the paned windows and lace curtains are only vague clues as to what awaits inside. Those who know, don't let on.

Chez Daniel is an intimate, very sophisticated, very French restaurant owned and operated by Daniel Rigollet. He also prepares its cuisine. Chef Daniel is a member of the world's oldest guild for masters of cuisine, the Confrerie de la Chaine des Rotisseurs; his meals are the culmination of his culinary experience in France, Switzerland, Germany, Ireland, and the Netherlands.

Daniel combs the Victoria markets early each morning to obtain his high-quality ingredients. His prevailing attitude: continually strive toward perfection. The charming, gracious chef uses only the freshest foods, and the quality is evident in his dishes.

Two candlelit dining rooms, each decorated in a muted pallette of mauve and teal, accommodate an intimate number of diners. Baroque music and rich kitchen aromas create a pleasing atmosphere. Guests are greeted warmly; the waitstaff upholds the finest standards of service, delivering a cheery "Bon appétit" with the commencement of your meal.

Very Fresh, Very French

Begin with one of Chez Daniel's appetizers such as fresh sauteed mushrooms, escargots with garlic butter, sweetbreads with mushrooms and port in a puff pastry, or Beluga caviar. Daniel's "soup a l'oignon, au gratin" is a fresh rendition of the traditional soup. Salad with hearts of palm and artichoke is the perfect intermezzo before the main course. "Salade Ceasar" is artfully prepared at your table.

Daniel's broad selection of entrées may make it difficult to choose just one. Salmon with Noilly Prat and cream and fresh trout with almonds lead the fish section. Fresh prawns, sautéed in butter and topped with tomato and a dash of garlic is another popular selection. A special "Rable de Lapereau 'Hussarde'" (loin of rabbit) is prepared for parties of two, and young rabbit in a white wine sauce is a delectable alternative. Fresh lamb with a ginger, shallot, brandy, cream sauce is one of Daniel's favorites, as is breast of pheasant, deglazed with port, Madeira wine, diced apple and mushrooms and a light cream topping.

Chez Daniel's extensive wine list includes some 125 selections from Australia, California, Canada, France and Germany. Fine champagnes (Dom Perignon and Perrier Jouet Brut) round out the cellar.

Homemade fresh fruit sorbets are an excellent, light finale. A tray of cheese, mostly imported, is offered in keeping with the French tradition. The dessert tray is hard to resist, though, with its chocolate truffles, creme caramel Chantilly, and tartelette au fruit.

A potpourri of teas, including various herbal blends, and espresso cap off the evening. Chez Daniel also serves a variety of dessert "special" coffees, including the Chez Daniel café, with five liqueurs, and a choice of select cognacs and digestives.

Getting There

Take Fort Street from downtown Victoria until it becomes Cadboro Bay Road. Continue to Estevan Avenue. Turn right and continue three blocks. The restaurant will be on your left in a row of shops.

Daniel Rigollet is both chef and host.

SOOKE HARBOUR HOUSE

Address:	1528 Whiffen Spit Road, Rural Route 4, Sooke, B.C. V0S 1N0
Telephone:	(604) 642-3421 or 642-4944
Location:	23 miles west of Victoria
Hosts:	Fredrica and Sinclair Philip
Room Rates:	Approximately $35 to $173 (U.S.)
Credit Cards:	American Express, Diners Club, MasterCard, Visa
Remarks:	Breakfast and light lunch included in room rate Reservations Recommended

If ever an inn was created to lull life's tempo back to a natural adagio, it's Sooke Harbour House. A trim, white farmhouse, this elegant inn rests just above Sooke Harbour's Whiffen Spit. Broad views of the Straits of Juan de Fuca and Washington's Olympic Mountains are seen through the inn's picture windows. Below, an ever-changing landscape of tidal pools, kelp beds, and natural driftwood sculptures create a living mural.

Stitching the many fabrics of Sooke Harbour House together are Fredrica and Sinclair Philip. Fredrica, born in Cannes, France, radiates a refined warmth. Dressed in her crisp French frocks, she graciously manages the workings of the inn as well as the raising of their four children. Sinclair, a native of Vancouver, holds a doctorate in economics from the University of Grenoble, where he and Fredrica met. He is well-studied in wines and foods, and an expert Northwest seafood chef.

World Class Dining

Colorful gardens ring the inn. Although it may seem odd to see Sinclair snatch a crimson petal from a poppy and take a bite out of it, guests themselves are soon enough nibbling on pansies, pineapple sage, Corsican mint, or any of the gifts from the inn's 400 varieties of herbs, flowers, berries and fruit trees — over 95% of the gardens on their grounds are edible, and most of it ends up on the menu. The ocean realm, too, offers prodigious harvests of delicacies such as octopus, sea urchin, gooseneck barnacle, periwinkles and whelks. Under the spell of Sooke's masterful chefs, the land and sea gardens blend to create the freshest and most innovative cuisine in British Columbia. Ann Hardy's renowned national guidebook *Where to Eat in Canada*, has just awarded the inn's restaurant three stars as one Canada's top eight restaurants.

Skin Dives Daily

"Here, when we say seasonally, we mean daily," says chef Pia Carroll. Pia, born and raised in England, is a member of the "Chaine des Rotisseurs" and a master gardener. Sinclair, an avid scuba diver, harvests the rich bounties of their watery front yard for the evening's meal. The inn's commercial fishing boat supplies fish and crab to create a menu that changes daily. Sinclair,

Fredrica and Sinclair Philip serve only the freshest available foods.

Fredrica, Pia, and Ron Cheri share the chef''s duties. Each is an artist with food as their medium.

Fresh sea urchin roe and fresh sea cucumber may appear as appetizers. Fresh steamed sablefish with an anise-hyssop butter sauce, or fresh skate sautéed with a cranberry vinegar sauce may be among the choice of entrées. More traditional seafood dishes are always available, as well as local, organically grown meats such as rabbit, veal, lamb, duck, guinea hen, venison and suckling kid.

Ideal For Honeymoons and Romance

Sooke Harbour House, like its cuisine, is an exquisite mingling of traditional French country sensibilities and West Coast native design. The New House, completed in 1986, offers ten distinctly different, definitely divine rooms. Each is named and decorated with a theme. All have an expansive ocean view and private balcony or terrace. In each room, a comfortable sitting area faces a fireplace which is made and ready to be used.

One of the most coveted rooms of the assemblage is the Victor Newman Longhouse, named for the Sooke carver of its many Indian masks and rare hand carved Chieftain's bench. This large room features a king-size bed and whirlpool for two. The whirlpool is situated next to a see-through fireplace, that lends a view of Sooke Bay and the mountains beyond. Outdoor whirlpools are found on the decks of the Mermaid Room and the Octopus's Orchard. Both have stunning views through their own private gardens by the ocean. The Icthyologist's study, sometimes referred to as the "Fish Room," is a veritable aquarium of fish art, including hand painted fish tiles, fish prints, fish rubbings, and fish weavings. As in many of the other rooms, hand painted tiles

Some of the new rooms have a hot tub on their private porch.

are also found in the Edible Blossom Room, where taking a shower is really a botany lesson in disguise.

The Sooke Harbour House bears all the charm of an airy French auberge. The five bedrooms in the old house are furnished with antiques, handmade flower wreaths and handsewn quilts. The split-level Blue Heron features a king-size bed, spacious sun deck, and perhaps the best view from the Inn.

Whiffen Spit, Beaches and Trails

To explore the Sooke Harbour House's world of wonders, begin with a walk along Whiffen Spit. Bald eagles nest nearby, while herons, sandpipers, loons and cormorants frequent the area. Killer whales, seals and sea lions feed just offshore as well as the "resident" year-round grey whale. The inn's staff will arrange for scuba diving, kayaking, or windsurfer and fishing charter rentals. Nature walks can be arranged with ethnobotonists, or local guide and bilingual staff member, Michel Jensen-Reynaud. The area is ideal for photography; horses nearby and the inn's bicycles are also available for rent.

The West Coast Life Saving Trail and Pacific Rim National Park begin near Port Renfrew and extend nearly 100 miles along the coast, offering excellent hiking opportunities. Surfers ride the waves at nearby Jordan River.

Getting There

From Victoria, follow Highway 1 North to the Highway 14 intersection. Follow signs to Sooke. Approximately one mile from the stoplight in Sooke, turn left onto Whiffen Spit Road. Follow it to the water, where the Sooke Harbour House is on your right at the ocean's edge.

HASTINGS HOUSE

Address:	P.O. Box 1110, Ganges, B.C. V0S 1E0
Telephone:	(604) 537-2362, reservations (800) 661-9255, from Western Canada and the United States
Location:	Salt Spring Island, Canadian Gulf Islands
Host:	Louise Harker, Manager
Rates:	$180 to $330 double, $160 to $270 off-season (Canadian). Each additional person $25. Breakfast and afternoon tea included.
Credit Cards:	American Express, MasterCard, Visa
Remarks:	Minimum stay of two nights on weekends in July and August; three nights on holiday weekends. No guests under 16. Closed January.

Hastings House is located on 25 acres of Salt Spring Island's thickly forested, lushly meadowed land. An adult retreat of the highest caliber, it bears a striking resemblance to an English farmhouse. Designed and built in 1942 by Warren Hastings, a naval architect, it is, in fact, a replica of the home he remembers from his childhood in Sussex.

Six handsome buildings comprise the country estate — the largest, the white half-timbered Manor House, is the focal point. Leaded glass windows, beamed ceilings, wooden floors and antiques, along with soft classical music, create an elegant atmosphere. Upstairs, a library nook and two seaview suites await, each with two bedrooms and full bath. Manor West overlooks Ganges Harbour, while Manor East overlooks the garden where fragrant English roses climb outside the windows. In the living room a huge inglenook contains a cowled, brick fireplace. Afternoon tea is served here. Sharing the main floor is the dining room.

The most deluxe suites are located in the Farm House, overlooking the bay. Farm House East and West both have king-size beds upstairs and a sitting room with open fireplace downstairs. Two full bathrooms and a front and back porch are found in both suites.

Post Cottage, the first Hudson's Bay Post on Salt Spring Island, is situated under a pear tree in the nearby orchard. Wicker furniture, a wood stove, and floral batiks accent the cozy cabin. French doors open onto manicured lawns. Just beyond the Cottage is the Barn, which features two parlor suites and two guest rooms.

Cliff and Ivy are the newly added accommodations. Located, appropriately, on an adjacent bluff, the Cliff Suite features a king and a twin-size bed, as well as a large living room. Ivy, downstairs from Cliff, is a one-room suite.

Each suite has a wet bar, refrigerator, fireplace and private telephone. Down quilts, fresh flowers, oversized towels and deep, plush carpets enhance the luxurious atmosphere. Manager Louise Harker is nearby to attend to every

Enjoy dinner in the Manor House dining room.

detail. The staff, mostly longtime islanders, takes special note of each guest's name and needs, making certain everyone feels welcome.

Hastings House appeals to discerning travelers seeking luxury and privacy in a natural setting. It is not uncommon to see deer wandering through the gardens, birds clustered around the feeders or seals feeding off shore. Hastings House is also a noted conference retreat. The Mews conference facility, outfitted with audiovisual equipment, accommodates up to 20 people. The staff works to ensure productive meetings by attending to every need. Full meal and beverage service may be arranged for your group. An accompanying spouse activity program is available.

Special Touches

The pampering begins the moment you arrive. A personalized nameplate appears on the door to your room and a thermos of hot coffee or tea arrives with fresh baked goods in a quilted hamper each morning. Your dinner menu presents your selection in beautifully hand-drawn calligraphy. While you dine, your room is straightened, the fire laid, and fresh towels put out.

Dining in the Manor House is as much a treat as staying in the accommodations. Award winning three- and five-course dinners create a true dining adventure. Chef Steven Lynch skillfully prepares what he deems "California Continental." Menus change daily, assuring long term visitors a change of pace. Steve utilizes herbs and vegetables grown on the estate and local seafood, as well as imports from Hawaii, New Zealand, and the North Atlantic. A French influence is evident in the delicate sauces, while an occassional Oriental spice sneaks into his cuisine as well.

Post Cottage was the first Hudson's Bay Post in the area.

Dinner is served at 7 p.m. and a table must be reserved prior to 1 p.m. of the same day. After dining, guests are invited to retire to the living room for coffee and liqueurs by the stone fireplace. (Warren Hastings buried an earthenware pot under the hearth here to ward off witches, according to Sussex custom.)

Breakfast is served in the dining room to guests only. A la carte luncheons and Sunday brunch are open to the public.

Tranquil Island

Salt Spring boasts a "cool Mediterranean" climate due to favorable Japanese currents, so there are many year-round activities here. A tranquil atmosphere prevails at Hastings House and on Salt Spring Island, and guests are encouraged to relax in the peaceful solitude. Hastings House itself offers the use of rowboats and croquet equipment; boat rentals, fishing, sailing, golfing, tennis and bicycling are just minutes away.

The town of Ganges, a mere five-minute walk from the estate, is lined with excellent galleries and shops. Local artisans are known for oil and watercolor paintings, pottery, carvings, weavings and stained glass. A farmer's market each Saturday, a salmon derby, jazz festival, and golf tournament are further ways to enjoy the island. Hiking and beachcombing are always popular pursuits. Picnic lunches may be requested for all-day excursions.

Getting There

Salt Spring Island is serviced daily by B.C. ferries from Tsawwassen, Swartz Bay and Crofton. Louise will arrange to pick you up from the ferry if requested.

THE OLD HOUSE RESTAURANT

Address: 1760 Riverside Lane, Courtenay, B.C. V9N 8C7
Telephone: (604) 338-5406
Hosts: Michael McLaughlin and Ferdinand Bogner, Owners
Cuisine: Continental
Prices: Entrees $10.95 to $17.95 (Canadian)
Hours: 11:30 a.m. to 9 p.m. daily, upstairs dining room
                 opens at 5:30 p.m. and is closed Sunday and Monday
                 (Monday in summer only) Sunday brunch served
                 10:30 a.m. to 2 p.m.
Remarks: Reservations strongly recommended in summer.

The town of Courtenay, in the vast Comox Valley, is situated mid-way along Vancouver Island's eastern flank. The Courtenay River meanders through the valley, its mild waters passing farms, mills and homes. In 1938, along the river's then wild banks, the pioneering Kirk Family built their home on four acres of the loveliest land in the valley. In 1973, it was purchased by Michael McLaughlin and transformed, over a matter of six months, into a premier dining spot — The Old House Restaurant.

"At the Old House," says Mike, "we aim to create an all-around enjoyable experience, which includes the grounds, buildings and people. Food is the primary reason people come here, but the surroundings certainly enhance the whole feeling."

Tradesmen used huge fir timbers and weathered wood gathered from old homes and barns in the area to renovated the home. Shingled and gabled, The Old House blends rugged West Coast architecture with the touches of an elegant home, creating a warm and intimate dining experience.

The Old House is essentially two restaurants sharing one roof. Entering on the ground floor, one is reminded of a lively English pub. A stone fireplace and heavy beams lend a lodge atmosphere which is popular with aprés-ski and aprés-anything crowds. Meals are moderately priced, and feature robust pub-style sandwiches, salads, pastas, and local seafood specialties.

Upstairs at the Old House one finds a more elegant dining room, lit with coal-oil lanterns and warmed by a fire. Open timbers are accented by skylights and hanging plants. Leaded windows offer views of the river and the grounds surrounding the restaurant. White linens, candles, and fresh flowers complete the tastefully appointed room.

Specialties of the House

Chef Ferdinand Bogner gleans the finest of local ingredients to create his array of dishes. The seasonally changing cuisine reflects an artistic presentation of delicious foods. Begin the meal with a soup such as Cream of Pheasant and Black Beans (with wild mushrooms, cranberry cream, and a touch of gin). Salads are innovative as well—the Butter Lettuce and Scallop Seviche salad is embellished with oyster mushrooms, scallions, pinenuts, and a raspberry vinagrette. The Old House's entrees may include Medallions of Reindeer, Prawns with Black Spatzle, or a specially prepared Partridge dish. An extensive wine list features European, Canadian, and American vintages to provide the perfect complement to any meal.

The Old House offers lunch selections such as gourmet salads, soups, sandwiches adn intriguing items like Seafarer's Schnitzel and ploughman's traditional pub fare. Sunday brunch is a feast ranging from Honey Glazed Camenbert with Almonds to Seafood St. Jacques.

On the Grounds

The beautifully manicured grounds are ideal for a stroll following a meal. An outdoor deck is a prime dining spot in warmer months. A small gazebo, on the river's bank, offers a place to watch seals, otters and blue herons. Weddings are held here, as is summertime entertainment. Just behind the restaurant is Dover Cottage, offering jewelry, gifts, home decorations, and collectibles.

Getting There

From Nanaimo, drive north on Highway 19. Entering Courtenay, turn right on 17th Street. Before crossing the bridge, turn right again on Riverside. The Old House is just ahead on your left. Allow one and one-half hours from Nanaimo.

The elegant Old House is on the bank of the Courtenay River.

APRIL POINT LODGE

Address:	Box 1, Campbell River, B.C. V9W 4Z9
Telephone:	(604) 285-3329
Location:	On Quadra Island, off Campbell River on the northeastern coast of Vancouver Island
Hosts:	Phyllis, Warren, Eric, Carl, Mark, Joy and Troy Peterson
Room Rates:	$109.50 to $149.50 (Canadian), $25 each additional person. Guests under 16 stay free. Two- and three-bedroom suites from $295; three- to five-bedroom guest houses from $325.
Credit Cards:	American Express, MasterCard, Visa
Remarks:	All meals — à la carte except packages. Open May 1 through October 15

The phrase "Nice fish" echoes across Discovery Passage, bounces off Vancouver Island, and lands firmly on the dock at April Point Lodge where you have just unloaded a bounty of shimmering salmon. For here, in the waters off the Campbell River, you have just discovered what veteran anglers knowingly refer to as "legendary fishing."

April Point Lodge is a world-class resort that stretches along three and one-half miles of shoreline on Quadra Island. Over 200 acres of coastal forest lands surround the main lodge and its guest cabins. Constructed by the Peterson family in 1944, the lodge is still run by brothers Eric and Warren, and their lively 77-year-old mother, Phyllis. Today's refined lodge emerged from the original set of ramshackle dwellings on what had been called Poverty Point. It continues to have worldwide appeal to fishermen and retreat seekers alike.

The handsome main lodge is the communal gathering place. It houses the dining room, lounge, office, and a handful of guest rooms. Suites within the lodge feature a living room, fireplace and sun deck. Spacious studios in the main lodge and guest lodges, as well as two- to five-bedroom cabins, are available. April Point's lodgings all offer a view of the water and private bath. Some include a fireplace, kitchenette and hot tub.

Total Fishing

From May through late September, the nurturing waters around April Point are obliging host to meaty salmon, cod and perch. Early season yields bluebacks, or immature Coho, which continue to grow until mid-September when they may weigh up to 22 pounds. Chinook are in large throngs by late May, and escalate to as much as 40 to 60 pounds by mid-summer. Fishing carries well into September; chum salmon may surface as late as mid-October.

April Point maintains the largest privately owned fleet of Boston Whalers (about 45) in the world. Ranging from 13 to 21 feet in length, these swift craft carry guests from the lodge's docks into the abundant waters of Discovery Passage, the Campbell River, and Seymour Narrows. The staff of 50 highly

Spacious suites all have expansive water views.

experienced guides are what make the fishing fun and fruitful. With strong hands-on experience, and a thorough development program at the lodge, these guides rank among the most respected in British Columbia, if not the world. In addition to vast knowledge of fishing techniques, they are well versed in local history, Indian fishing methods and food preparation, safety, and marine life management.

Generally, guides fish with the guests for the duration of the week. Guided trips cost $35 to $40 per hour for two people, with a four hour minimum. Cost includes the boat, guide, tackle and fuel. It is customary to tip the guide, either daily or at the end of the week. The week's catch may be frozen and packaged for travel, or a local firm will can or smoke it for you.

Fresh Air Appetites

A day of fishing, or just breathing the fresh salt water air, builds a healthy appetite. Fortunately, April Point prides itself on quality dining. The fresh seafood selections are naturally extensive, and change daily depending on local catches. Dungeness crab, served cracked with drawn butter, is a standard item. Prawns, ling cod and snapper are frequent bestsellers, as is, of course, salmon. Should you choose, the kitchen will prepare your very own salmon, in a festive fashion, and serve it to you in the dining room for a minimal fee. Rack of lamb and prime rib, as well as outdoor steak barbeques round out the entrées. Lunches are primarily soups and sandwiches, while breakfast is simply not breakfast without one of "Mrs. P's" stickie buns.

The dining room, with its Northwest Coast Indian masks and cedar beams, overlooks Discovery Passage. At night, freighters and cruise ships pass by, while in the daylight seals, whales and eagles may be seen. Guests gather in

Large private decks come with many of the suites.

the cozy bar before dinner to swap fishing tales, and around the fire afterwards to set the records straight.

Beside the Point

Quadra Island boasts a strong Indian heritage which bears exploration. One of the oldest original Kwakiutl Indian villages lies near the lodge and has a fascinating historical museum. At Cape Mudge an ancient petroglyph site is well worth the visit. Rebecca Spit, on the east side of the island, offers stunning mountain views. Beachcombing, clam digging, oyster picking, swimming and hiking are accessible from the lodge. Boat tours may also be arranged.

The kitchen will prepare a gourmet picnic hamper for you and your guide to enjoy on a beach, complete with linens, silver, and fine wine. Cracked crab or Cornish hens are two of the movable feasts.

The Petersons can arrange a guided hike to discover many of the Indian Petroglyph sites, some of which are only found at low tide. For a real surprise ask about "swimming with the salmon" in the Campbell River.

Getting There

To reach April Point by car, drive 160 miles north of Victoria to Campbell River. Take the Quadra Island ferry, which runs nearly every half-hour. Follow Pidcock Road to the lodge. To fly, scheduled air service is available from Vancouver to Campbell River, then take water taxi or limosine service to the lodge. From Sea-Tac airport in Seattle, you can make arrangements with Lake Union Air to pick you up at the airport and drive you to Lake Union where their seaplanes are moored. From there it's a two-hour flight directly to the lodge.

PARK ROYAL HOTEL

Address: 540 Clyde Avenue, West Vancouver, B.C. V7T 2J7
Telephone: (604) 926-5511
Location: In West Vancouver, just north of the Lion's Gate Bridge
Host: Mario Corsi, Manager
Room Rates: $74 to $185 (Canadian)
Credit Cards: American Express, Carte Blanche, Diners Club, MasterCard, Visa
Remarks: Coffee or tea and morning newspaper delivered to room, complimentary.

"The Park Royal is a country style inn found in a busy metropolis," says host Mario Corsi. "It's cozy, and has a staff who really care about the comfort of the guests." Mario should know; after all, most of his staff have been with him for a good part of his 15 years as manager of the hotel. Mario's European upbringing and hotel training have led him to create a high standard of service and quality reminiscent of a Continental hotel. "Nothing phony or glitzy," he says proudly. "Just a good feeling, like being in a little village. The problem with lots of hotels these days is that there is no surprise." That philosophy and Mario's enthusiasm are what make the Park Royal such a rare find in a city of more than 1.2 million. This hotel is delightfully different.

Located on the north side of Vancouver's harbor, just minutes from the bustling downtown area, the Tudor style, ivy festooned hotel provides a quiet retreat for the business or vacation traveler. The two-story building is surrounded by trimmed lawns and flower beds. The Capilano River runs just outside. Twelve of the inn's 30 rooms face the river and overlook the gardens. On quiet nights you can open the window and be lulled to sleep by the rushing water. Most rooms offer queen or double beds; a few have twins. All rooms have private baths, and are individually decorated with floral print wallpapers, antique oak furniture, and leaded glass windows. A large suite offers a jacuzzi, VCR, plush terry robes and a wet bar. (Future plans call for the addition of more rooms of this caliber.) The morning newspaper and coffee or tea are delivered to your room upon request. These are just a few of the touches that lend Park Royal its intimacy.

An authentic English pub downstairs offers lively piano entertainment Monday through Saturday evenings. The piano player has been playing at the pub for years despite his youth, and is rarely ever stumped when you call out a request. Pubsters may just be tempted to belt out a favorite melody in this intimate lounge.

Public rooms are paneled in dark woods. Flowered and scenic print draperies hang on the windows. A big stone fireplace, set with a crackling fire, is especially cheery on a damp Vancouver evening in winter.

The elegant Tudor Room overlooks the gardens.

Consistent Quality

Park Royal is as proud of its restaurant as it is of its rooms. The Tudor Room is regarded as one of the top dining spots in the city. Regional specialties and old standards combine to create a diverse menu with wide appeal. Hans Schaub, chef here for 12 years, prides himself on freshness and consistency of product. The dining room overlooks the garden, and is warmly appointed with tapestry-covered chairs, vintage prints and stained glass. Dinner entrées include breast of pheasant with red currants and brandy, black pasta with smoked salmon, red caviar and cream, and traditional favorites such as beef Wellington and Châteaubriand. A resident baker supplies fresh breads and stunning desserts.

Breakfast and lunch selections are as noteworthy as dinner. Begin the day with huevos rancheros or eggs Park Royal (poached eggs, smoked salmon, salmon caviar and Hollandaise sauce). Lunch offers a steak and kidney pie, scallops in a fresh basil cream, or veal scaloppine.

Herbs from the inn's year-round greenhouse are used in the cuisine, giving a bright, fresh taste. In warm weather, lunch, cocktails and snacks may be taken on the secluded patio off the dining room.

Exploring the "Other" Vancouvers

Park Royal is located in West Vancouver, just a few minutes walk from the Park Royal Shopping Center. Over 190 shops are found in this trendy mall, including three of Canada's top department stores: The Bay, Eaton's and Woodward's. Ambleside Park stretches along the shore behind the mall, and may be reached by following a trail outside the Park Royal Hotel.

Lawns and gardens are on the bank of the Capilano River.

North Vancouver offers additional opportunities for exploration. Grouse Mountain is a favorite destination in any season. Two aerial tramways depart for the mountaintop every 15 minutes, 10 a.m. to 10 p.m., offering spectacular views of the city and environs. Mountain meadows, paved walking paths, and the Blue Grouse Lake and nature trails offer excellent hiking for all fitness levels. In winter, four double chair lifts and two T-bars carry skiers to the 4,100-foot peak. Helicopter tours are available for reaching even greater heights. To get there, take Marine Drive to Capilano Road. Head north on Capilano to Grouse Mountain.

En route to the mountain, visit the Capilano Suspension Bridge and Park. Constructed of wire rope with wood decking, the bridge stretches four hundred and fifty feet across the canyon, some two hundred and thirty feet above the river. At night, illumination adds to the spectacle. Crossing the bridge you may view Coho and Chinook salmon on their upriver swim to the Capilano Hatchery. The west side park contains trout and salmon ponds, historical and botanical trails.

North Vancouver's newest waterfront attraction is Lonsdale Quay Market. A bustling public market with boutiques and shops, restaurants and cafes, the area also offers a prime view of Vancouver and the harbor.

Getting There

Follow Georgia Street through Vancouver across the Lion's Gate Bridge. Take West Vancouver Exit. Turn right onto Clyde Avenue. Go one block. Turn right, the hotel is on the left. Free parking is available.

CORSI TRATTORIA

Address:	1 Lonsdale, Vancouver, B.C. V7M 2E4
Telephone:	(604) 987-9910
Hosts:	Mario and Antonio Corsi, Owners
Cuisine:	Italian
Prices:	Entrees $6.95 to $13.95 (Canadian)
Credit Cards:	American Express, Diners Club, MasterCard, Visa
Hours:	5 to 11 p.m. daily.
Remarks:	Reservations recommended.

Corsi Trattoria, located on North Vancouver's waterfront across from the new Lonsdale Quay Market development and the SeaBus to downtown Vancouver, offers Italian cuisine in an authentic Mediterranean atmosphere. A bright green awning outside yields to the white stucco and terra cotta inside. Burgundy and pink linens, candles and photographs lend a cozy feeling. "You can go in blue jeans or a long gown," says co-owner Mario Corsi. "You can bring your girlfriend or your grandmother."

The Brothers

The Corsi brothers, Mario and Antonio, have been in the restaurant and hotel business since their childhood, when their family ran a small hotel outside Rome. "It's not just our business," Mario says,"it's our life."

Both brothers are involved in the restaurant, and Antonio is chef. "He is always in and out of the kitchen talking to guests," says Mario.

"It's simple, the way a trattoria should be," says Antonio. "We put our effort into the food, service and atmosphere and work at making everyone feel at home."

A Classic

Corsi Trattoria blends the finest of central Italian cuisine with the freshest of West Coast ingredients. Ever conscious of fine ingredients, the restaurant orders its veal from a special source in Montreal. Fish and fowl are carefully selected from local markets.

Classic dishes include a wide variety of antipasto, as well as over 50 pasta specialties. Fettuccine, gnocchetti, spaghetti, fusilli, bucatini and capelli d'angelo are among the pastas made fresh daily on the premises. Featured entrées are penne all'Arrabiata (spicy tomato sauce with bacon and Romano cheese), and spinach fettucine with cream, ham and mushrooms.

For lunch, you might have antipasto of mozzarella in carrozza (fried mozzarella in tomato sauce), rotollo a las Corsi (pasta stuffed with spinach, ham and cheese), pasta salad with shrimp or steamed clams.

Beyond Pasta

Though Corsi Trattoria is noted for its pasta dishes, the menu extends far beyond. Traditional Italian entrées are beautifully prepared and served with attention rivaling that given the pastas. Non-pasta dishes include prawns, pan fried in butter and sprinkled with oregano and white vermouth, or a veal scallopine in an apple and cream sauce. Fritto misto (lightly breaded fried prawns, mussels and squid) is also a popular dish, as is breast of chicken laced with dried mushrooms and proscuitto. Accompanying vegetables arrive perfectly *al dente* on side plates. Dinner salads include spinach and mushroom, mixed greens or fresh mozzarella and tomato.

For dessert: creme caramel, zabaglione and zoccotto, an Italian chocolate cake are a few of the options. An almost entirely Italian wine list offers selections in many price ranges.

A Roman Orgy

The most popular item on the menu is a feast of five different pastas in an array of sauces (minimum of two orders). "L'Abbuffata" includes four different pastas, a mixed salad, lamb, veal piccata, prawns, zabaglione and espresso (also a minimum of two orders).

Getting There

Go east on Marine to Lonsdale. Turn right. The restaurant is located on the last right corner. The Lonsdale Quay's ICBC lot offers plenty of parking nearby.

Antonio Corsi makes 50 types of fresh pasta each day.

THE TEAHOUSE RESTAURANT

Location: In Vancouver's Stanley Park at Ferguson Point
Telephone: (604) 669-3281
Host: Brent Davies, Owner; David Richards, Felix Zerbuchen, Maitre D's; Margaret Olney, Day Manager
Cuisine: Continental
Prices: Brunch entrees $8.25 - $12.95, lunch entrees $7.75 - $9.45, dinner entrees $12.95 - $16.95 (CND)
Credit Cards: MasterCard, Visa, American Express
Hours: Lunch 11:30 a.m. - 2:30 p.m. Monday - Friday; dinner 5:30 - 10:30 p.m. Monday - Saturday (until 9:30 p.m. Sunday); Saturday brunch 11:30 a.m. - 2:30 p.m., Sunday brunch 10:30 a.m. - 2:30 p.m. Open daily except Christmas Day.

On the map, Vancouver's hand reaches up to cradle the busy Burrard Inlet. On the tip of its thumb is Stanley Park — 1,000 acres of ornamental gardens, towering forests and rolling lawns. On the park's west side, commanding a view of English Bay, is Ferguson Point and the Teahouse Restaurant.

During World War II, Ferguson Point was a military installation, with the present day Teahouse serving as garrison and officers' mess. Following the war, the buildings were first used as a residence, then as a small scale summer teahouse. Needing repairs, it was closed in 1976 by the city. Present owner Brent Davies, a Vancouver native, leased the decrepit structure from the Parks board, renovated it, and opened it as a restaurant in 1978.

The original building was comprised of what is now the entrance area and Tea Room. In 1980, the Conservatory was added, followed two years later by the Drawing Room. Painted in what Brent calls "teahouse green" all three areas are comfortably decorated in a tapestry and wicker motif. Palms and chrysanthamums grace each room. The glass enclosed Conservatory, warmed by a fireplace, is a cozy place for observing freighters or Canada geese on a winter day. The Drawing Room and Tea Room, too, offer splendid views of English Bay and the distant Coastal Range on Vancouver Island.

More Than Tea

The Teahouse serves weekend brunches as well as daily lunches and dinners. The cuisine far surpasses the connotation of a "teahouse" in its variety and presentation. The waitstaff, dressed in kilts and pressed shirts, deliver pleasant and precise service; the table is set with fresh linens and clear crystal.

Lunch may begin with an appetizer such as a hot, delicate mousse of fresh prawns topped with red caviar sauce, or a homemade paté with white wine and spices, green peppercorns and hazelnuts. A daily soup, as well as a hearty Fisherman's Soup, are always on the menu. A variety of full-meal garden plates (Duck Salad or Terrine of Salmon and Scallops) are available, as are enticing hot luncheon dishes such as Chicken Andalousia (sliced chicken breast, red pimentos, black olives, tomatoes and mushrooms flamed with Cognac and cream) or Scallops aux Fonds Artichauts.

Dinner's menu is an expanded version of the luncheon menu, with specialty items such as rack of lamb, roast duck, veal, pheasant, salmon, prawns, scallops and fresh fish of the day. There are also daily creations left to the chef's creativity. Desserts are made fresh on the premises and include baked Alaska, sherry trifle, chocolate marquise. All are accompanied by a selection of dessert wines, Teahouse coffees and, of course, tea. An extensive wine list features French, Italian, Spanish, Californian and Australian selections. Please note that the Teahouse Restaurant does not serve high tea. The name of the restaurant was kept for historical reasons.

In the Park

A myriad of recreational facilities are found in the park, including pitch and putt golf, swimming beaches, tennis courts, a zoo, an aquarium, and a summer theater under the stars. While the park is most popular in spring and summer, winter is a fine time for a drive along the forested roads.

Getting There

The Teahouse Restaurant is located at Ferguson Point in Stanley Park between Second and Third beaches. From north and west Vancouver, take the Lion's Gate Bridge south. Immediately after the bridge take the Prospect Point/Park Drive Exit and continue through the park to the restaurant. From downtown Vancouver, take Georgia Street to the same exit.

Diners face the water in Stanley Park.

THE WILLIAM TELL

Address:	765 Beattie Street, Vancouver, B.C. V6B 2M4
Telephone:	(604) 688-3504
Host:	Erwin Doebeli
Cuisine:	Swiss Continental
Prices:	Lunch entrees $7.75 to $10.75, dinner $18 to $23. (Canadian)
Credit Cards:	American Express, Diners Club, MasterCard, Visa
Hours:	Lunch 11:30 a.m. to 2 p.m. Monday-Friday; dinner 6 - 10 p.m. daily.

The legendary folk hero William Tell is traditionally known for his tremendous strength and skill as a marksman — particularly when it came to shooting an arrow through the apple on his son's head. He represents the spirit of the movement toward Switzerland's independence, and is esteemed for his strength of character. In his honor, Swiss born Erwin Doebeli created Vancouver's William Tell Restaurant with the same high standards and spirit of independence.

Doebeli began his restaurant career in Switzerland, holding positions in every aspect of the trade. Emigrating to Canada in 1962, he continued to develop his knowledge and experience and opened the William Tell Restaurant in 1964. Over the years the menus changed, the locale improved, and the kitchen was modernized. In its near quarter-century of operation, the William Tell has achieved and maintained ratings as one of the finest restaurants in Vancouver.

The restaurant's impeccably dressed and well-trained staff deliver excellent service, while Doebeli himself circulates the dining room to greet guests and ensure their satisfaction.

The original restaurant was located on Richards Street. A couple of years ago it was moved to its much larger, more elegant quarters in the Georgian Court Hotel. A formal air of sophistication and worldliness prevails. The three cream-colored rooms have comfortably spaced tables covered with Swiss linens, oversized silver service, plates, and delicate fresh flower arrangements. Embossed napkins, silver flatware, and the large menus all bear the William Tell insignia, a crossbow motif. A stained glass window with Swiss crest looks out onto the Expo '86 stadium across the street.

Swiss Precision

William Tell's food and service are as carefully detailed as the decor. Chef Kurt Kuhn insists on the finest ingredients, and delivers a premium product. Five- and three-course *prix fixe* menus are offered in addition to the à la carte selections. These reflect seasonal variations and showcase new items. The restaurant's cuisine had, several years ago, been classified as conservative. The new kitchen perhaps brought about a new outlook— its renderings are lighter and more imaginative than its predecessor.

The à la carte selections appeal to all tastes and appetites. Upon seating, complimentary puff pastries filled with salmon mousse are served. Hors d'oeuvres range from air-dried, Swiss style beef to leek and smoked goose breast in puff pastry. Salads are fresh and innovative, a favorite being "La Salade du Marché" (or today's choice from the market), which could be smoked pheasant or perhaps goose paté on curly endive.

A selection of fish, fowl and meats comprise the two-page entrée listings, including a filet of salmon in sorrel sauce, medallions of monkfish and prawns in saffron, and marinated rack of lamb with garlic and fresh herbs. Entrées are accompanied by tender vegetables from the nearby Granville Market or other favorite foraging spots. Sea asparagus and miniature vegetables are but a few of the unique offerings.

The lunch menu stresses soups, salads, and a choice of entrées ranging from Pacific salmon with pink peppercorn sauce to broiled filet mignon in a lively mustard sauce.

Getting There

From Vancouver's Georgia Street, heading east, turn right onto Cambie Street. Turn left on Robson, then take another left onto Beatty. The restaurant is in the Georgian Court Hotel directly across from B.C. Place on the Expo '86 grounds.

Erwin Doebeli will be your host.

LA BROCHETTE

Address:	52 Alexander Street, Vancouver, B.C. V6A 1B4
Telephone:	(604) 684-0631
Hosts:	Dagobert Neimann, Chef, Owner; Pierre Carrat, Restaurant Manager
Cuisine:	French Country
Prices:	$14 to $24 (Canadian)
Credit Cards:	American Express, MasterCard, Visa
Hours:	6 to 10 p.m., Monday through Saturday, lunch served during December.

La Brochette, located in a quiet corner of Vancouver's historic Gastown District, has achieved distinction as "a connoisseur's restaurant." It has a loyal following of Vancouverites, but has also been recognized by nationally known gourmets as a superb world-caliber restaurant. "One of the secrets," says owner Dagobert Neimann," is the slow cooking method we use over our antique tournebroche."

Vintage French Rotisserie

It is this tournebroche, painstakingly imported by Dagobert Neimann, that propels La Brochette into a class of its own. The massive 16th-century vertical wood grill with rotating spits dominates an entire wall of the restaurant. It is said to be the only original French rotisserie utilized in a North American restaurant. Lamb, veal, pork and duck are slowly grilled in a manner that preserves their succulent juices and flavors. "We are aware that this method is slower, but we believe it is also infinitely superior," says Dagobert.

Dining at La Brochette is not a matter of just eating a meal; it is an event. While the open fire seductively grills meat and poultry on the mid-level, a massive woodburning fireplace warms the lower. The small and intimate restaurant is perfectly designed for leisurely dining: there is no turnover so the table is yours for the entire evening.

Dagobert, born in Bavaria where his grandparents owned a hotel, was trained in Switzerland and Germany. His commitment is to a "light, uncluttered and direct approach to cooking."

In keeping with this dedication to quality, the restaurant stocks nearly 300 vintages of fine wines: German, Alsatian, French, Californian, Oregonian, Australian, South African and Canadian. The staff, many of whom have been with the restaurant since its opening nearly ten years ago, are treated to an annual tour of one of the world's wine regions. The result is a staff well versed in wines and most able to assist in finding the appropriate accompaniment to any meal.

Intriguing Choices

The only difficulty at La Brochette will be selecting from the many menu items. The hors d'oeuvres list is extensive and varied, including a delicate hot paté of scallops, prawns and sole; a grilled filet of snapper in tomato, jalapeno and pepper sauce; crepe of lamb with pineapple and cream curry sauce; or steak tartare. Salads range from simple Boston lettuce with marinated mushrooms to exotic hot duck liver with bacon and mushrooms on a bed of lettuce, and topped with raspberry vinegar dressing. Duck consomme with oyster mushrooms and quail egg, and shellfish bisque with Pernod are among the soup selections. Veal medallions with morel, meadow and black oyster mushrooms in a demi-glace sauce with brandy, broiled filet mignon flambéed with black peppercorn sauce, and Fraser Valley duckling roasted on the spit, flambéed with calvados and served with apple cream sauce are but a few of the entrées.

Every meal begins with a complimentary basket of crudités, and is served with fresh vegetables prepared in an imaginative fashion. Uncommon vegetable dishes, such as braised lettuce or beet root, are often available. A tray of cheese is served a troom temperature, and an array of desserts concludes the meal. In keeping with La Brochette's high quality, the desserts are worth succumbing to the temptation.

Getting There

From Harbour Centre, go three blocks along the waterfront in Gastown.

Dagobert using his 200-year-old rotisserie.

HATHEUME LAKE RESORT

Address:	P.O. Box 490, Peachland, B.C. V0H 1X0
Telephone:	June through September, have operator connect you with area code 604 operator and ask for Kamloops Radio – Merritt channel, then ask for Hatheume N699408. (604) 767-2642 off season
Location:	About one and one-half hours by unpaved road west of Peachland or east of Quilchena
Hosts:	Tim and Janet Tullis, Gus and Leni Averill
Room Rates:	$155 per day, $1,000 per week (Canadian) American Plan. Children from five to 12 are charged at two-thirds rate
Credit Cards:	None
Remarks:	Reservations necessary.

Over the years, as trails and roads sliced farther into the interior of British Columbia, fishermen discovered a remote pocket of lakes known to native Indians as Hatheume, or "Big Fish." Of all fresh water game fish, none holds quite the reputation for size and fighting spirit as the Kamloops trout, a hardy strain of rainbow found almost exclusively in the isolated lakes that dot the forested Nicola Plateau, a high plateau wilderness situated between the Coastal Range and the Canadian Rockies. There's something about these thick woods and cold lakes that mends the soul. For those seeking peace and quiet in a remote setting, Hatheume Lake Resort is an excellent choice.

A Wilderness Retreat

Among the straight pine and quaking aspen along the shore of Lake Hatheume, you will find a splendid lodge and six comfortable cabins, all built of hand-hewn logs. For a few days, a week perhaps, guests can become part of the penetrating freshness of this rare wilderness. Each of the eight lakes that together make up the Hatheume Lake Resort still support resident loons and occasional deer, bear and moose can be seen as well.

The exuberant greeting from Gus Averill or his wife Leni is as genuine as the trout jumping out there in the lake. Then again, it may be Tim Tullis who comes from the dock to welcome you, or his wife Janet. That bottle of Okanagan wine in your cabin is just one of the ways they have of saying they're glad you've made it. Until the moment you leave, they and their very competent staff will do everything they can to make sure you're comfortable and content. The Averills and Tullises have plenty to do just keeping the equipment running and the meals coming, but they always seem to find time to give a fly casting lesson, brew a fresh pot of coffee or suggest spots for photography.

Clean and Homey

The facilities are basic, clean and homey. Each of the well-heated cabins has two large bedrooms with twin beds, a private bath with shower and a nicely furnished sitting room which looks out onto the lake. The cabins are arranged

Belly boats are also provided.

to assure privacy; you can sit on your covered porch and see nothing but the water, hear nothing but the call of the loons. In the lodge, you can prop your feet on the raised hearth of the huge circular fireplace and read or chat or nap.

Each morning Gus or Tim brings coffee to your cabin, a gesture that ensures everyone makes it to breakfast. Janet and Leni prepare tasty and varied meals, served ranch style with more than enough for everyone at the table. Over sausages, hotcakes and hash browns, everyone decides on the day's fishing spot. Large lunches are already packed. Four-wheel drive vehicles are ready for you to take to one of the outlying lakes, where you'll find sturdy wooden boats equipped with outboard motors, boat cushions, anchors, nets and tackle boxes. Gus and Tim point you in the right direction, from there, it's up to you. Choose a different lake each day of your stay.

Cooperative Trout

The eight lakes provide plenty of variety, and only guests at the resort have access to them. Jerry and Rouse lakes are the most remote, perhaps the most scenic, and often yield the most fish. Fishing is consistently good. Because of the abundance of feed in these cold, spring-fed lakes, the trout commonly reach one to three pounds, and there is the opportunity to catch trophy fish. The fish aren't finicky either; just about any fishing method results in a good catch. Gus and Tim can't recall anyone who left empty-handed.

Seldom do non-fishermen feel left out; guests can follow their own paths, content with the absence of pressure, of responsibility, of things that must be done. Hatheume has a fleet of mountain bikes available for day or evening rides or for working off a hefty meal.

The lodge faces Hatheume Lake.

At the end of the day guests gather together again for dinner. It might be ribs or roast, veal cutlets or turkey, served with heaping plates of fresh vegetables and freshly baked rolls. Everything, including dessert, is as hearty as it is delicious. Evenings are peaceful and sleep comes easily.

Making Plans

This is a destination resort, so a holiday here requires thoughtful planning. Write early, ask questions, make your reservations. You need to remember that even during the hot summer months the temperature at this altitude (4,600 feet) can be brisk, especially at night. Come prepared for the odd rain storm.

Most guests return again and again because they can depend on the hosts to be as cooperative as the fish. When your stay has ended, you may be reticent about packing your gear and starting your car again. Just take your fish (which can be frozen or smoked for your convenience), your photos, your memories and begin thinking about next year.

Getting There

From Vancouver, take Highway 1 eastward to Hope, then take the new Coquihalla Highway to Merritt. Continue on Route 5 through Quilchena about one-half mile. Turn right onto a gravel road marked Pennask Lake. Follow the signs to Hatheume, about two hours distant. Or, travel Highway 97 to Peachland. At the stoplight turn west to Brenda Mine (approximately 16 miles). As you approach the mine turn left on a gravel road and follow signs for about 20 miles to Hatheume Lake. Allow a couple of hours for a leisurely drive to the lodge.

Redfish Lake

Idaho

Idaho has a particular air that brings us back here time and time — one that's fresh and clean and authentic. Lightly scented with evergreen, it is alive with the chatter of pine squirrels in morning and gently interrupted by a loon's cry at night. In Idaho, eagles, elk and bighorn sheep live naturally in wide open spaces. We both feel a litle more relaxed whenever we are in the state which is as often as possible.

Idaho is river country. The Snake, Salmon, Clearwater, Middlefork,Payette, Selway, Lochsa, and Wood Rivers are but a few of the thousands of watery fingers caressing the state's spiny back. They roar and tumble down craggy peaks, meander through foothills, then drift across plateaus and plains, pausing in languid lakes. The 16,000 miles of rivers and 2,000 lakes are meccas for white water rafters, kayakers, and fishermen.

Just as Idaho is river country, it is also mountain country. Within the 83,000 square mile state lie 200 peaks of 8,000 feet or more, some reaching as high as 12,000 feet. The Tetons, Sawtooths, and Lost River Range (Idaho's tallest) provide a full gamut of activities from hiking to snowshoeing, and horseback riding to skiing.

Idaho's Indian Nations

Idaho's 10,000-year-old Indian heritage is strong and rich. Vestiges of the colorful past remain today in the place names, traditions, and in descendants of the native peoples. For the most part the tribes lived in peace until the white man unsurped their land and wars became more frequent. Three major Indian wars were fought in Idaho, forcing the Indians to move to reservations.

Indian petroglyphs, often called rock writing, are scattered over much of Idaho, primarily in the Snake River area. One way to view petroglyphs is on a white water float trip in the wilderness area. Five tribes can be found today in the state: Kutenai, Coeur d'Alene, and Nez Perce reside in the north, with the Shoshone-Bannock and Paiute in the south. Indian exhibits, dances, games, parades, and feasts are often held on the reservations or at State Fairs.

Basque Country

Idaho is home to the largest concentration of Basque people in the United States, with over 20,000 Basques residing in the Snake River plain and in the Boise/Mountain Home area. The Basque culture is very intact. Customs and language have been proudly and faithfully preserved. One of Idaho's unique offerings is a performance by the Oinkari Basque Dancers. Many Idaho communities have traditional Basque celebrations each year.

The Gem State

Legend holds that the state's name was derived from an Indian word "E Dah Hoe", which translates roughly to "gem of the mountains." The theory was disproved, yet the name stuck, and with good reason. Idaho is a rock hound's haven. Star garnets, diamonds, jasper, agate, sapphires and rubies are among the more than 80 varieties of gemstones unearthed within the state's borders.

National Parks, Forests and Recreation Areas

Idaho is fortunate to have two most congenial neighbors: Yellowstone and Grand Teton National Parks. Both parks, although not officially in Idaho's boundaries, are within easy driving distance from eastern Idaho.

Hells Canyon National Recreation Area spans 652,488 acres of prime northern Idaho wilderness straddling the Snake River. Hells Canyon is the deepest gorge in North America, towering 9,300 feet above the river in spots.

Sawtooth National Recreation Area, in the two-million acre Sawtooth National Forest, is a vast recreational paradise. Over a half-million acres of land provide year-round enjoyment. Fishing, boating, rafting, hiking, skiing and horseback riding are among the popular sports. Sun Valley, home of the world's first ski resort, offers challenging skiing and limitless recreation.

The Salmon River, the mythical "River of No Return," carves a path of sheer cliffs and crashes down from its Sawtooth source in turbulent rapids. The Middle Fork of the Salmon and the Salmon Wild and Scenic Rivers offer white water river running. Fishing for trout and steelhead, and big game hunting are among the highlights of the Salmon National Forest, P.O. Box 729, Salmon, ID 83467 (208) 756-2215.

Idaho boasts several other national forests, including Targhee National Forest in the southeast, with its towering peaks reaching 11,000 feet; the Nez Perce, in central Idaho, with terrain ranging from flat plateaus to steep canyons; and the Challis National Forest, where four major mountain ranges lie and the Middle Fork of the Salmon Wild and Scenic Rivers runs.

Craters of the Moon National Monument, has upwards of 80 square miles in central Idaho, presents a haunting landscape. Lava beds punctuated with brittle cinder cones lend a rather unearthly feel.

Weather

Idaho's climate lends itself to year-round activities. During summer, nightly lows average from 45 to 60 degrees Fahrenheit, daily temperatures range from 75 to 95 degrees. Summer tends toward dry and warm, while winter brings cold yet comfortable temperatures and moderate snowfall.

Liquor Laws

Legal drinking age in Idaho is 19. Liquor is sold in state liquor stores or by the drink in bars which close at 1 a.m. Liquor is not sold on Sundays or legal holidays.

Information Sources for Idaho

Idaho Travel Council
Statehouse
Boise, Idaho 83720 (208) 334-2470 in Idaho

Selected Idaho Events

January
Winter Ski Carnival— Sandpoint
Basque Sheepherder's Ball — Mountain Home
Winter Fest — Sun Valley

February
Busterback Stampede (Cross Country Ski Race) — Stanley
Winter Carnival — Salmon
30k Boulder Mountain Ski Races — Sun Valley

March
Sawooth Derby (Cross Country Ski Race) — Stanley
Idaho State Champion Cutter and Chariot Races — Pocatello

April
Bald Mountain Closes For Skiing — Ketchum

May
Salmon River Rodeo — Riggins
Music Week — Boise

June
River Trips on Snake River Through Hells Canyon, Middle Fork of the
Salmon and Bruneau Canyon — Hughes River Expeditions
National Old Time Fiddler's Contest and Festival — Weiser

July
Hailey Rodeo — Hailey
Basque Picnic — Boise
Snake River Stampede and Festival — Nampa

August
Arts and Crafts Festival — Sun Valley
Wine Auction — Sun Valley
Northern Rocky Mountain Folk Festival — Hailey

September
Wagon Days — Ketchum
Annual Basque Dinner — Hailey
Twin Fall Country Rodeo — Filer

October
Basque Carnival — Boise
Shoshone-Bannock Indian Day — Fort Hall

November
Bald Mountain Open For Skiing — Ketchum
Holiday Parade — Boise

December
Christmas Eve Torchlight Parade and Caroling — Sun Valley

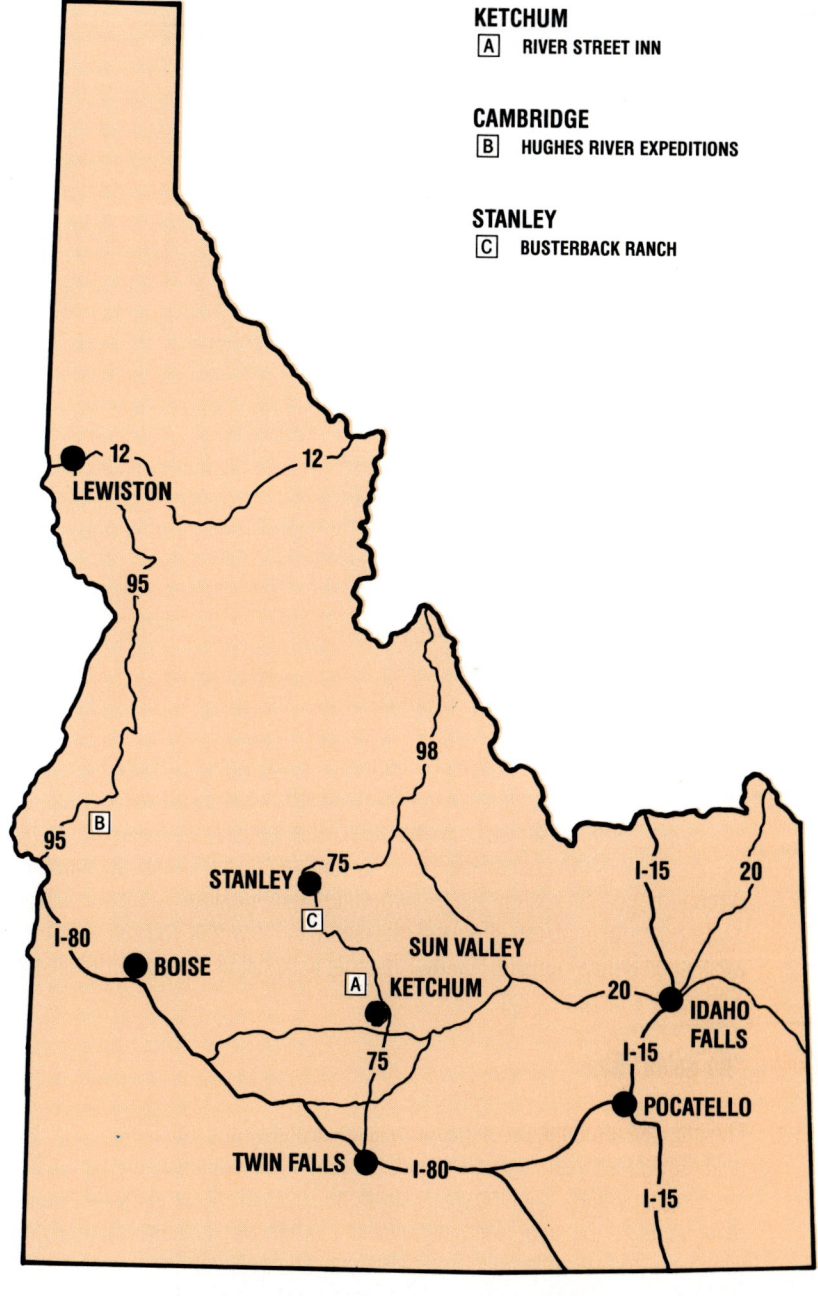

KETCHUM
A RIVER STREET INN

CAMBRIDGE
B HUGHES RIVER EXPEDITIONS

STANLEY
C BUSTERBACK RANCH

12
LEWISTON
12
95
98
95
B
STANLEY 75
C
SUN VALLEY
I-80
A KETCHUM
I-15 20
BOISE
20
IDAHO FALLS
75
I-15
POCATELLO
TWIN FALLS I-80
I-15

RIVER STREET INN

Address:	100 River Street West, Ketchum, ID 83340
	P.O Box 182, Sun Valley, ID 83353
Telephone:	(208) 726-3611
Location:	On Trail Creek in southern Ketchum
Hosts:	Ginny Van Doren, Bonnie Barclay
Room Rates:	$85 to $125 double (spring, summer and fall) $10 additional in winter; discounts for extended stays, single and commercial rates available
Credit Cards:	American Express, MasterCard, Visa, Discover
Remarks:	No smoking in bedrooms

Neatly tucked on a quiet street just a few blocks from the core of Ketchum, River Street Inn is a pleasing blend of friendly warmth and respectful privacy. Its innovative architecture melds the charm of turn-of-the-century Victorian sensibilities with the open, airy spaces of contemporary Western design. Palladian windows, polished brass and whitewashed oak combine to create a soothing environment.

The spacious living room is dominated by a natural brick fireplace above which hangs a massive grapevine wreath woven with eucalyptus branches and dried flowers. The comfortable colors of the parlor seating — sage green, ivory and dusty rose — invite you to linger over a cup of tea.

From the living room, French doors open onto an expansive deck. Cottonwoods and aspens border Trail Creek which runs just below. The deck provides an ideal spot for early morning bird watching or late night star gazing.

The eight guest rooms are really more like guest suites. Decorated in soft prints and pastels, they furnish queen-size beds, walk-in showers, small refrigerators, and Japanese soaking tubs, the perfect panacea for weary muscles. Six of the suites face the rocky tumble of Trail Creek. Its soothing symphony coaxes restful sleep. Two suites overlooking mountain vistas invite peaceful contemplation and relaxation. In the winter you can watch the weather on Bald Mountain, "Baldy," in order to best time your departure to the slopes for a day of skiing.

"No Rules" Rule

The intimate atmosphere of the inn was co-owner Ginny Van Doren's special goal. Seventeen years ago, Ginny left her job in San Francisco and found her heart in Sun Valley. Over the years, she honed her skills by working for several restaurants in the area. Her experience led to her own success formula, one which she and reservationist Bonnie Barclay share. River Street Inn's secret: let the guests set the tone. If you wish to visit over a cup of coffee in the kitchen, the more the merrier. However, if privacy is your goal, it is most assuredly

THE

RIVER STREET INN

BED AND BREAKFAST

GINNY VANDOREN ⬩ PROPRIETRESS

All rooms have a queen-size bed, refrigerator and a Japanese soaking tub.

respected. Ginny and Bonnie are available for friendly conversation or to assist in any arrangements or information you need to enhance your stay.

River Street Breakfast

Breakfast at River Street Inn is an indulgent feast which will carry you well through lunchtime. Begin with fresh fruits, juices, coffee or tea. Dive into one of Ginny's homemade baked Danish rolls or coffeecake. A special entrée, one of Ginny's surprise concoctions, follows: ricotta pancakes, frittatas, spinach and sausage puff pastry, or German apple pancakes are among her favorites. Ginny's "no rules" rule means breakfast may be eaten on your own schedule. As she says, "Breakfast is from 8 to 10, unless guests want it earlier or later, or in bed."

In winter, skiers gather for "après ski" in the inn's living room. Home baked cookies are served with tea. Beer and wine are also available. In summertime, iced tea is served on the deck.

Down in the Valley

Ketchum and Sun Valley are situated in the narrow Wood River Valley. Sun Valley is most noted as a skiers haven. Imposing Bald Mountain hovers over the town. Baldy has 16 chair lifts and over 64 runs on its 3,400 feet of vertical drop. The area offers some of the most challenging skiing in the country, yet has appeal for skiers at all levels of expertise. Sun Valley's expert staff of ski instructors is nationally acclaimed. A free shuttle runs from just across the street from River Street Inn to the base of River Run. Nordic skiing is popular in the valley, and local outfitters will arrange backcountry trips for skiers in search of unbroken powder.

Breakfast can be taken on the deck overlooking Trail Creek.

Summer and fall visitors have the opportunity to see yet another side of Sun Valley's personality. The high desert climate is warm, dry and dependable. The fall is a patchwork of colors as aspen trees go through their yearly changes. A full line-up of sports are available including horseback riding, bicycling and hiking. River Street Inn's guests receive a special discount at the Warm Springs Tennis Club. Four golf courses in the valley entice expert and duffer alike. There are special guest privileges at the new million dollar athletic club just one-half block away as well. A view of the valley is best seen by hot air balloon or the Hailey Airport gliders. Just south of Hailey, Magic Reservoir awaits waterskiers and windsurfers alike. Wood River Valley is also home to some of the best trout fishing streams in the country. Ketchum's many fine shops entice shoppers who browse for year-round sport clothing as well as furs and leather goods. The town offers many fine restaurants with selections ranging from natural foods to elegant Basque or French cuisine.

North of Ketchum is a cemetery where a simple slab marks Ernest hemingway's grave. Farther out on Trail Creek, in the heart of hte country he called home, you'll find the Hemingway memorial. On it is written: "Best of all he loved the fall... the leaves yellow on the cottonwoods, leaves floating on the trout streams and above the hills the high blue windless skies." you will understand why.

Getting There

Fly into Hailey Airport, south of Ketchum, and take a taxi or rental car to the inn. Heading north on U.S. 75, turn left at River Street, just beyond the Trail Creek Bridge. The inn is two blocks toward the mountains, on your left. There is plenty of private parking in front of the inn.

HUGHES RIVER EXPEDITIONS

Address: P.O. Box 217, Cambridge, ID 83610
Telephone: (208) 257-3477
Locations: Snake River through Hells Canyon, Middle Fork
of the Salmon River, Bruneau, Owyhee and
Salmon River Canyons
Hosts: Jerry Hughes and Carole Finley
Credit Cards: None. Personal checks accepted
Remarks: Member of Idaho Outfitters and Guides Association

Adrenalin-rushing rapids. Deep gorges and open back country. Sun drenched days and star drenched nights — a river expedition with Hughes is all this and more. The small, owner-operated company specializes in the rivers of Idaho and Eastern Oregon, and prides itself on personal service, expert professional guides, excellent equipment, and providing a memorable river experience.

Owner Jerry Hughes utilizes his 23 years of river life to create the high standards of Hughes River Expeditions. He and his veteran crew know the rivers and canyons well.

The National Geographic Society has on five separate occasions chosen Jerry Hughes and Carole Finley to be its outfitter and guide for the rivers in this region. "Ours is a family business that is as much a lifestyle as it is a way to earn a living," says Jerry. "We both feel strongly that a first class outfitting business cannot be a big business, so we limit the size and scope of our trips to ensure our personal attention to each trip's organization and planning."

Variety of Boats

The river boats, including inflatable kayaks, paddle and oar boats, and McKenzie drift boats, are custom rigged for navigating challenging rapids. The outfitters provide tents, waterproof gear packs, foam-lined camera boxes, ground tarps, sleeping bags and pads, dining tables, and camp chairs. All gear is hauled by 22-foot supply rafts.

The camp work and cooking is taken care of for you on this first-class expedition. Fresh meats, vegetables and salads feed hungry paddlers. A Dutch oven means freshly baked goods are available, and plenty of ice is carried to ensure you have chilled pop, beer or dinner wine.

The Rivers

The Snake River/Hells Canyon trip features powerful, big wave rapids, as well as fine fishing for small mouth bass, rainbow trout and channel catfish. Hells Canyon is the deepest canyon in North America, a staggering 7,900 feet at one point. The area is rich in history, including more than 8,000 years of habitation by the Nez Perce, Shoshone, and Sheepeater Indians. Pictographs, rock shelters and house pits are among the archaeological treasures visited. Pioneer homesteads and mines are also on the agenda.

The Middle Fork of the Salmon River is Idaho's most famous white water river. It descends rapidly among rugged peaks and heavy forests, past sage-covered slopes and between sheer granite cliffs. This series of rapids makes the river a classic. "Blue Ribbon" trout fishing (catch and release), beautiful campsites, natural hot springs and Indian and pioneer sites create a diverse and interesting experience.

The Owyhee River crosses the Owyhee Plateau, forming the longest back country river system in the Northwest. It meanders between basalt cliffs past juniper thickets, lush hanging gardens and slopes covered with fragrant wild flowers. Antelope, beaver, otter, Canada geese and bighorn sheep may be spotted here. The mighty rapids on this river create one of the most formidable river expeditions in the West.

Bruneau Canyon winds through the West's most dramatic desert canyon where sheer walls tower above the river. Five Mile Rapids offer one of the most famous white water stretches in Idaho. Salmon River Canyon is most noted for fall steelhead fishing. Comfortable drift boats are used here for a dry ride. The "River of Return" offers quiet pools and surging rapids for a challenging ride.

Getting There

Directions will be given to the starting point at the time of booking.

Boats are matched to the safety requirements of each river.

BUSTERBACK RANCH

Address: Star Route, Ketchum, ID 83340
Telephone: (208) 774-2217
Location: Forty miles north of Ketchum on State Highway 75
Hosts: Logan Largent, Resort Manager; Jeana Leavell, Lodge Manager; and Bill Leavell, Winter Manager
Room Rates: Full American Plan, two days one night $125 with private bath, $110 shared bath; three- to six-night packages available; complete ski package, modified American Plan, rates available. Lunch and dinner served to non-guests.
Credit Cards: MasterCard, Visa
Remarks: Rates include three family style gourmet meals and cross-country trail pass, skis and instruction.

Busterback Ranch is a year-round resort and working cattle ranch 40 miles north of Sun Valley. Like a pearl in a jagged oyster shell, Busterback rests in Idaho's Stanley Basin between the Sawtooth and White Cloud Mountain ranges. Its eastern boundary is the Salmon River, otherwise known as the River of No Return.

"John Breckenridge owned the ranch just before I did," owner Dr. Lee Enright explained. "His father homesteaded the place in 1910 and sort of carved the ranch out of the sagebrush. Breckenridge had a small cabin over by Petit Lake and his wife used to say 'If you keep coming up here and workin' so hard you're going to bust yer back.'" Well, the name stuck, and eventually the main ranch was known as Busterback. For today's guest, however, life is anything *but* bust yer back.

Mountain Mecca

Busterback's assemblage of log buildings is a mecca in the broad Stanley Basin. Situated on 2,700 acres, it commands a view of the entire valley. A main lodge houses the community living area, a kitchen and five guest rooms. At night it glows with candlelight and firewood warmth. The living room is comfortably decorated with oak chests, plush sofas and an antler candelabra. Near the etched front door of the ranch house, a hand written scroll depicts the history of Busterback Ranch.

Each of the ranch house bedrooms is individually appointed with Indian rugs and animal skins, peeled log furniture and brass fixtures, thick comforters and crisp linens. Lace ruffles adorn the queen and twin beds. Two rooms offer private baths; three share. Three neat log cabins, Alpine, Alturas and Toxaway, sit just off the main house and offer quality, secluded accommodations. The Western motif continues here in the woodman's plaid comforters, peeled log furniture and wood burning stoves.

Adjoining the main house is the recently added White Cloud Lodge. With its tall, stone fireplace and long dining table, this comfortable room accommo-

There is lots to do after a refreshing night's rest.

dates Busterback's day visitors. Overnight guests can also enjoy mingling here, yet retain the privacy of the main lodge. The ranch house is rimmed by a large sun deck, an ideal spot for viewing the vast valley and sunbathing in Idaho's bold sun.

Guests dine family style around the kitchen's butcher block table. Bountiful breakfast spreads feature omelettes bubbling with cheese, ranch potatoes, egg quesadillas or orange pancakes. Fresh ground coffee, juices and fruits accompany the meal. There are a selection of homemade soups and delicious cookies for lunch. Dinners feature an exotic feast of delicacies created by Busterback's culinary wizards. Roast veal Dijon, seafood en brochette, Moroccan pasta, and roast leg of lamb in an herb marinade are a few of the entrées. Leafy salads, saffron rice or Idaho spuds are added to make a colorful table. A fine selection of wines and beers complement the meal. Scrumptious desserts follow, such as apple brie strudel, almond raspberry torte or banana flambé, so be sure to save room.

An aura of comraderie prevails as guests gather in the living room after dinner. The evening may close with piano or guitar music, a quiet view of a spectacular sunset, or a seasonal meteor shower.

Big Valley

The valley offers a spectrum of activities appealing to all levels of interests and abilities year-round. From the first snowfall through late spring, Busterback maintains 25 miles of meticulously groomed trails which begin just outside the back door. The trails vary in difficulty and length, so novice and expert alike are satisfied. Busterback's staff of fully qualified instructors are on hand to give lessons and pointers. A gear room stocks equipment in all sizes. Ski to one

The White Cloud Lodge adjoins the Main Lodge.

of the nearby lakes and drop into the 70-year-old sheepherder's wagon, now a warming hut, for a cup of tea. A local outfitter will arrange back country ski trips into the Sawtooth or White Cloud Mountains for day treks or overnight stays in a Mongolian style yurt.

Cross the Galena Summit to reach the world famous ski area of Sun Valley. Abundant Rocky Mountain powder snow falls here to make one of the country's finest downhill skiing areas. Novice and expert skiers choose from a broad selection of slopes. Instruction and equipment rentals are available.

Busterback's summertime complexion is that of an actual working cattle ranch. Two thousand head of cattle share the acreage. Guests are invited to watch the cowboys in action, but Busterback is not a "dude ranch," so joining in is not part of the curriculum. Horses are available for day trips into the Sawtooth National Recreation Area. Longer back country trips may also be arranged with local outfitters.

Float trips on the Salmon River are a favorite with summer guests, as are hiking, fishing and mountain bike rides. Busterback has canoes and windsurfers; horse and mountain bike rentals are available. After a full day of adventure you can return to Busterback for a hearty meal, a soak in the hot tub, or a bake in the Finnish sauna.

Getting There

Drive 40 miles north from Ketchum and Sun Valley on State Highway 75, crossing Galena Summit. Approximately six miles from the base of the mountain, watch for signs and turn right into the Busterback driveway.

Big Mountain

Montana

The sheer size of Montana is enough to impress Fred and me every time we venture into the state. The nation's fourth largest state, it spans 550 miles in length and about half that in width. Entering from the west, it's easy to see how the name Montana, the Latin word for "mountainous," came to be. Range after range of rugged Rocky Mountains appears around every bend. The vistas are unsurpassed — cascading mountain rivers, clusters of jagged peaks, lakes cradled like gems in a precious ring.

The grass plains of central Montana are home to the grand Missouri River and the famed artist Charlie Russell. A few maverick mountain ranges punctuate the sloping hills. To the east, we come upon the wide lands, where prairies stretch from horizon to horizon. After traversing Montana's 275-mile middle, we see how appropriate its nickname "Big Sky" really is.

Gold West Country

Montana's southwest corner is named the "Gold West Country" because it offers the restored remains of the state's gold rush days. It is the site of the somber Big Hole Battlefield National Monument, where Chief Joseph and the Nez Perce fought the U.S. cavalry in 1877. It is also home to famous fishing rivers and the long, graceful arm of the Bitterroot Valley. Virginia and Nevada Cities, on MT 287 out of Yellowstone National Park, are two old mining camps of the gold rush days which have been authentically restored. Here, one can recapture the feeling of post-Civil War days when large numbers of gold seekers were drawn upriver and overland to the West.The ghost town of Bannack, west of Dillon on Route 278, is the site of Montana's first serious gold strike. It was here, too, that Lewis and Clark made the decision to turn west to cross the Continental Divide.

Helena is the site of much history. In 1864 a gold discovery touched off a boom era that turned Helena into "Queen City of the West" and Montana's capital. The Original Montana Governor's Mansion, built in 1888, and St. Helena Cathedral, modeled after the cathedral in Cologne, Germany, are among the worthwhile stops. North of Helena on I-15 is the Gates of the Mountains, a 2,000-foot gorge along the Missouri River named by Lewis. A two-hour summer cruise introduces visitors to what he called the "most spectacular" gorge he had seen.

Land of Parks and Forests

Montana is a land of parks and forests. In fact, there are 10 state parks, 18 state monuments, and 71 state recreation areas in the state. Montana is the proud home to both Glacier and Yellowstone National Parks. Seventeen million acres of national forest and three million acres of untouched wilderness sprawl across the 93-million-acre state.

Seventy-five-year-old Glacier National Park is found in the northwestern corner of the state. Kandahar Lodge and Marina Cay are both close enough to make for easy exploring of Glacier. The Park is a brilliant masterwork of 50 glaciers and over 200 sparkling lakes. In 1974 the park was designated a World Biosphere Reserve by UNESCO to protect the park as one of the world's major ecosystems devoted to the conservation of nature and scientific research in the service of man. Glacier hosts about 200 grizzlies and a menagerie of other wildlife. Alpine meadows of vibrant flowers, dramatic waterfalls, awe-inspiring cliffs and dense forests are all a part of the parks panorama. Going-to-the- Sun Road cuts a 50-mile path east to west, crossing the Continental Divide and traversing the Garden Wall. It opens in early June and closes with October's snowfall. There are kokanee salmon spawning in lower McDonald Creek in fall; there is cross-country skiing in winter, and hiking in spring and summer, making Glacier a year-round destination. For information on the Park, contact: Superintendent, Glacier National Park, West Glacier, MT 59936 (406) 888-5441.

The National Bison Range in western Montana protects one of the most important herds of native bison left in America — 400 of these beasts inhabit the area's 19,000 acres of natural grassland. In addition, visitors will find many species of birds, herds of whitetail and mule deer, elk, bighorn sheep and pronghorns. The Bison Range is at Moiese, off U.S. 93 and MT 200 or 212. Phone (406) 644-2211.

Flathead Lake, the largest fresh water lake in the west, lies between Polson and Kalispell, offering nearly 200 square miles of prime fishing. It even has an island, Wild Horse, a 2,000-acre state park known for its bighorn sheep.

Yellowstone National Park is world renowned for its spouting geysers, crystalline pools and simmering mud caldrons. Rugged mountains and deep canyons are punctuated by flowing streams and calm lakes. All totaled, it is 2,221,000 acres of untamed wilderness. For information on the park, contact: Superintendent, Yellowstone National Park, WY 82190, (307) 344-7381.

The non-profit Yellowstone Institute offers some 50 field courses to help visitors gain a better understanding of the park and the way it operates. The courses last from one to eight days during the summer months. For a catalog and information, write: The Yellowstone Institute, Box 117, Yellowstone National Park, Mammoth, WY 82190, or phone (307) 344-7381, ext. 2384.

Historical Perspective

Montana's southeastern corner is called "Custer Country" for the Civil War general who got more Sioux and Cheyenne warriors than he bargained for. The Custer Battlefield National Monument, 15 miles south of Hardin off I-90, is the site of Custer's Last Stand, the spot where he and his troop of 225 men were lost in the 1876 battle.

"Charlie Russell Country" occupies the north-central region of the state. Named after the renowned Western artist, the area still boasts the hauntingly big and beautiful expanses he captured on canvas. Charles Russell Original Studio and House, preserved as it was in the early 1900s, still stands in Great Falls. The nearby museum features a collection of his oils. This part of the state also possesses the 149-mile portion of the Upper Missouri River, now designated as part of the National Wild and Scenic River System. A rare sample of primitive Montana wilderness, the area has not changed much since

Lewis and Clark came through in 1805. The Havre Badlands, northwest of Havre on Highway 233, are the site of many wonderful archaeological finds.

Family Retreats

Montana is family country. Wide open spaces and an equally broad selection of activities blend to create a naturally grand time for kids and adults alike. Dude ranch vacations offer families the chance to hike, bike, swim, wrangle horses, fish, fly kites, play softball or volleyball, walk, talk and then talk some more. Healthy ranch style meals are hungrily consumed; evening campfires and sing-alongs are a soothing end to an active day. Montana family retreats have a special way of bringing loved ones together, and creating memories that will long outlive the vacation itself.

Transportation

The major east/west highway in Montana is I-94, running from Glendive through Miles City to Billings. From there, it takes a slight turn northward and becomes I-90, continuing through Bozeman, Butte and Missoula. U.S. 2 is the northern route, accessing Glasgow, Havre, Glacier National Park and Kalispell. I-15 is the primary north/south route, running through Butte, Helena and Great Falls. The speed limit is 65 mph on major highways outside city limits. Seat belts are compulsory for all in the vehicle.

Amtrak services Montana with two routes. The "Empire Builder" serves Havre and Glacier Park, paralleling U.S. 2. Major airlines service Great Falls, Billings, Kalispell, Missoula, Butte, Bozeman and Helena.

Weather

Montana's weather is extremely changeable. Mountain temperatures plummet in the evening, and soar in the daylight hours. The most rainfall is during May, June and July. Precipitation the remainder of the year comes in the form of snow. Temperatures in July and August may range 60° to 90° Fahrenheit.

Liquor Laws

The legal drinking age in Montana is 19. Liquor may be purchased by the bottle in state licensed liquor stores and from bars.

Information Sources For Montana

Montana Promotion Division
Department of Commerce
Helena, MT 59620
toll free (800) 548-3390
(for general tourism information)

Montana Historical Society
225 N. Roberts
Helena, MT 59620

Montana Department of Fish, Wildlife and Parks
1420 East Sixth
Helena, MT 59620
(406) 444-2535
(for state park, historic sites, camping and fishing access)

USDA Forest Service
Northern Region
P.O. Box 7669
Missoula, MT 59807
(406) 329-3511
(national forest maps, wilderness maps, winter recreation)

U.S. Bureau of Land Management
22 N. 32nd St.
P.O. Box 36800
Billings, MT 59107
(406) 657-6561
(wilderness maps, off-road vehicle information, floater's guide)

National Park Service
c/o Grant-Kohrs Ranch National Historic Site
P.O. Box 799
Deer Lodge, MT 59722
(406) 846-2070
(national parks and historic sites)

Selected Montana Events

January
Pro-Rodeo Finals — Great Falls
Winter Carnival — Seely Lake
X-C Ski on Flathead Lake — Marina Cay Resort

February
Whitefish Winter Carnival — Whitefish & Big Mountain
Annual Winter Festival — West Yellowstone
Montana State Expo — Missoula

March
Doug Behers Winter Classic — Big Mountain
C.M. Russell Art Auction — Great Falls

April
American Ski Yachting Championship — Whitefish & Kandahar Lodge
Ski Golf Tournament — Big Mountain
Western Heritage Days — Missoula

May
Whoop-up Trail Days — Conrad
White Water Festival — Bigfork

June
Great Lake to Lake Canoe Races — Whitefish
Little Big Horn Days — Hardin
Whitefish Lake Run — Whitefish

July
Yellowstone River Boat Float — Livingston
Butte Vigilante Rodeo — Butte
Whitefish Arts Festival — Whitefish
Wild Horse Stampede — Wolf Point

August
Flathead Lake Sailboat Regatta — Bigfork
Montana State Fair — Great Falls
Northwest Montana Fair — Kalispell

September
Whitefish Summer Games — Whitefish

October
Bison Roundup — Moiese
Bald Eagle Gathering — West Glacier

November
Ski Season Opens — Big Mountain

December
Christmas Stroll — Bozeman
Anniversary Celebration-Christmas Torchlight Parade — Big Mountain

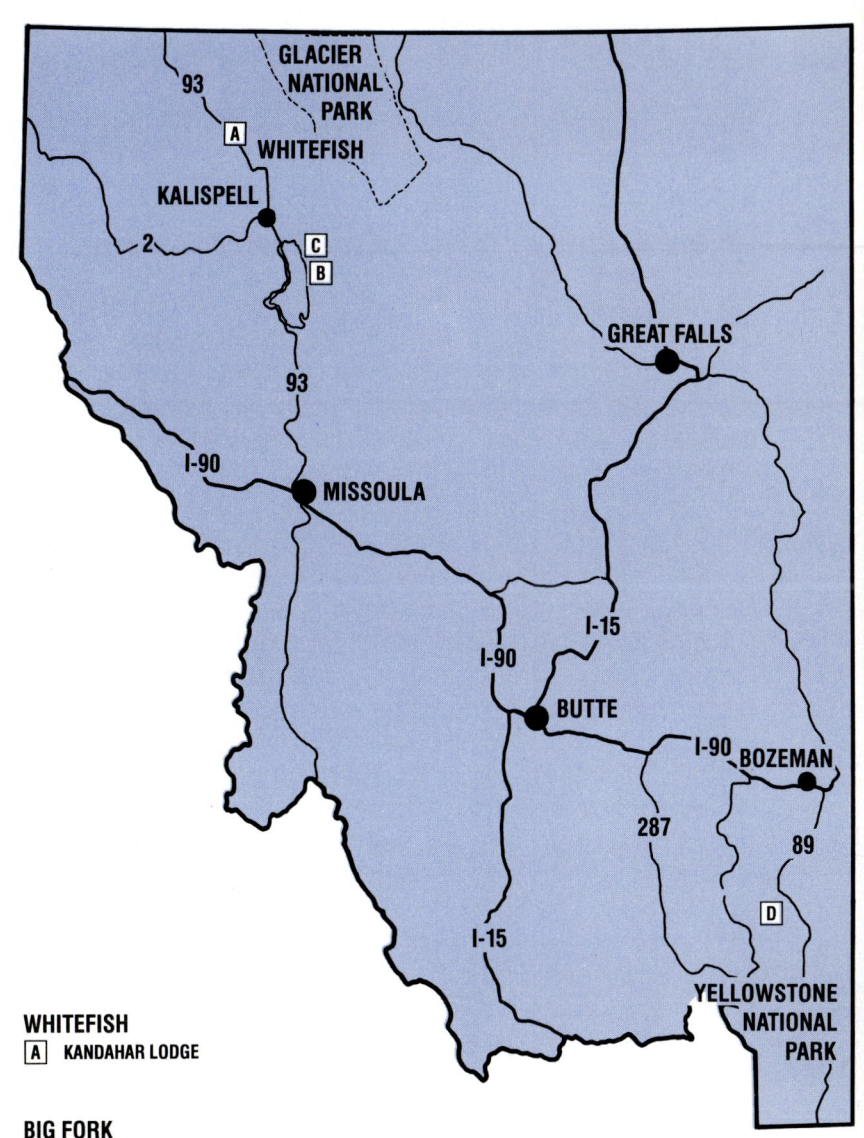

WHITEFISH
A KANDAHAR LODGE

BIG FORK
B FLATHEAD LAKE LODGE
C MARINA CAY RESORT

EMIGRANT
D MOUNTAIN SKY GUEST RANCH

KANDAHAR LODGE

Address:	Big Mountain Ski Resort Village, P.O. Box 1659, Whitefish, MT 59937
Telephone:	(406) 862-6098
Location:	On Big Mountain, eight miles north of Whitefish
Hosts:	Buck and Mary Pat Love
Room Rates:	$45 single, $58 double, $85 suites (summer); $66 to $132 rooms, $84 to $192 lofts, $160 to $208 two-room suites (winter). Weekly rates, season packages and one-bedroom apartment are also available.
Credit Cards:	American Express, MasterCard, Visa
Remarks:	Children under 15 stay free.

Kandahar, the story goes, is an obscure town in Afghanistan that was, in August 1880, the location of a besieged British garrison. British General Frederick Roberts marched to their rescue with 10,000 troops. He was knighted for his efforts and took the name Lord Roberts of Kandahar. Years later, as the vice president of an alpine sports club, Roberts lent his name to the trophy awarded the champion of the downhill racing event, and the Roberts of Kandahar Challenge Cup led to the creation of the Kandahar Ski Club, which sponsored the first international ski meet in which the winner is chosen on the basis of combined downhill and slalom race scores.

And so it came to pass that Buck and Mary Pat Love, two ski devotees with an admiration for the grand style of European ski lodges, named the alpine ski lodge in Whitefish, Montana, "Kandahar."

European Style Lodge

Mary Pat and Buck Love wanted to create an entire package: great skiing, beautiful scenery, and first class lodging and dining. From the start, they decided their priority was to spend as much time as possible with guests, to concentrate on making visitors feel at home and comfortable. They built their home as part of the lodge and are, in the best sense of the word, innkeepers.

Their "inn" is a three story European style lodge built around a central sunken lobby with an immense rock fireplace, an array of comfortable sofas and chairs flanked by reading lamps, a big screen VHS and upright piano. The walls are sided with knotty cedar and massive support beams. The entrance to the lodge has window arches and side panels of etched glass that display mountain and forest scenes by local Whitefish artist Myni Ferguson. On either side of the lobby, wide staircases lead guests to their second- and third-floor rooms, suites or lofts. Guests can reserve accommodations for one to eight people. Sixteen of the 48 units have small fully stocked kitchens. Enough kitchenware to cook a Thanksgiving dinner is provided, or the space can be used simply for storing drinks and snacks. The rooms have the same cedar paneling, sand colored carpets and color photos of skiing and sailing that decorate the lobby.

The lobby is a very comfortable place to gather and relax.

Skiers who return from the slopes of Big Mountain can ski right up to the front door of Kandahar, enter a heated boot room to remove ski gear, and walk in stocking feet to one of the two saunas, or to the jacuzzis for a long, slow dip into the 102° water.

After a Continental dinner in the Cafe Kandahar (specialties include sauerbraten mit katoffelklossen, chicken Maria, coquille St. Jacques and flounder Florentine), skiers and nonskiers alike can relax in the small lounge opposite the lobby, watch television, play cribbage or any of a number of board and card games. Although the lounge does not sell liquor, guests are welcome to bring their own.

Year-Round Enjoyment

Kandahar Lodge is open year-round and offers guests an assortment of activities. In the summer season (May to October), visitors can make the cool mountain resort their home base and take day trips to majestic Glacier National Park, the rugged Mission Mountains, the astonishingly blue Flathead Lake, and the nearby towns of Whitefish and Kalispell. For the outdoor enthusiast, there is bicycling, camping, boating and waterskiing, fishing, float trips, golf, hiking, hunting and windsurfing.

In April, the North American Ski/Yachting Championships take place on Big Mountain and Flathead Lake. For sailors who ski and skiers who sail, this event provides the perfect combination of mountain skiing and sailing on the nearly frozen waters of Flathead.

In the winter months (November to April), Big Mountain and the Kandahar Lodge are blanketed with fresh, powdery snow, so there is plenty of wintertime

Stairs lead to the spacious rooms upstairs.

fun, too. Eagle watchers flock to West Glacier to catch sight of the showy birds in October and November; Whitefish holds its annual Winter Carnival in early February; and snow lovers ride sleighs and chair lifts to pursue their sports. Cross-country skiers have miles of trails and roads to glide over, too.

One of the Best

Ski magazine called 6,770-foot Big Mountain "one of the best ski areas in the world." With 33 miles of ski terrain, 41 different runs and a daily skier capacity of 6,000, this claim is hard to dispute. There are five lifts, a T-bar and a platter lift. Daytime tickets cost $11 to $19.50; night skiing tickets (there are 53 acres of lighted runs) are $8. Private lessons are available from the Big Mountain Ski School.

Beyond the prices and the numbers, there is Big Mountain itself. The winter crisp air carries the clean scent of evergreens, and the view of the Flathead Valley is stunning. The practically nonexistent lift lines, even during the Christmas to New Year's crush, mean that Kandahar's guests can ski to their hearts' content in a place that satisfies their longing for adventure outdoors.

Getting There

Highway 93 North takes you alongside Flathead Lake through Kalispell and into Whitefish. In Whitefish, turn right onto Wisconsin Avenue (Highway 487) and follow the signs to Big Mountain. Kandahar Lodge is about eight miles north of Whitefish. Amtrak takes train travelers to the Whitefish depot, and buses and taxis ferry passengers to the mountaintop. Delta and Horizon airlines have daily flights just 45 minutes from the Lodge.

MARINA CAY RESORT

Address: 180 Vista Lane, P.O. Box 663, Bigfork, MT 59911
Telephone: (406) 837-5861, in Montana (800) 433-7836, elsewhere (800) 433-6516
Location: On Bigfork Bay, northeastern side of Flathead Lake
Hosts: Dan and Laurie Averill, Owners
Room Rates: $44 to $52 single, $68 to $78 suite, $120 to $200 apartments (one to three bedrooms) June 15 to September 5; $34 to $38 single, $42 to $46 suite, $48 to $98 apartments, September 6 to June 14. Monthly rates from $325 to $625 in off season.
Credit Cards: American Express, Carte Blanche, Diners Club, Discover, MasterCard, Visa
Remarks: No pets

On a quiet, cloudless summer evening, the moon rises over Bigfork. From the bayside decks of the Marina Cay units there is enough light to see fish rising to the surface of the water. Swan Mountain Range towers above the small town lights of Bigfork to the east. The moon's reflection on the water wavers as pleasure and fishing boats return to their berths for the night.

An Unfair Advantage

Marina Cay Resort is positioned on the west side of Bigfork Bay, where the Swan River empties into Flathead Lake, the largest body of fresh water in the west. This prime location gives Marina Cay an advantage that other resort owners would probably call unfair. Whether it's wildlife, water activities, mountains or streams, the Flathead has it all. Measuring 30 miles from north to south and 15 miles from east to west, Flathead Lake has 161 miles of shoreline and a depth of 386 feet.

The forested Swan Range and rugged Mission Mountains jut abruptly from the foothills to the east and southeast of the lake. The scenery of Glacier National Park to the north makes each visitor come away with a new sense of the meaning of "grandeur." The Flathead Valley is truly one of Western Montana's most scenic recreation centers.

Unique Accommodations

The Marina Cay complex was built five years ago, and consists of 85 units, a restaurant, lounge and marina. The beauty of the resort is in its unique mix of accommodations, from single rooms to a three bedroom suite with kitchen, living room, fireplace and patio. All rooms are decorated in soft pastels with bamboo and wood furniture.

A separate building houses the Cherry Tree Boutique, the Bay Club restaurant, and a full-service bar. This central area fronts the heated swimming pool and the jacuzzi.

The pool and hot tub are below the restaurant.

Full Day's Activities

Early in the morning is the ideal time for a stroll along the edge of Bigfork Bay. As you saunter over acres of manicured lawns and flower beds at the water's edge, you may even catch a glimpse of the sun peeking over the mountains to the east.

Spend your afternoon watching steady winds that kick up big, fluffy Montana clouds and send windsurfers skimming across the water, or head out onto the lake in pursuit of mountain bass, cutthroat, and lake and Dolly Varden trout. Fishing charters, complete with expert guides, take guests on half- or full-day trips on Flathead Lake, rivers or mountain lakes. In winter months, anglers can fish from heated ice houses. The managers know the best fishing holes and will gladly share their secrets with guests.

To show Flathead Lake at its best, Marina Cay rents canoes, fishing boats, ski boats, windsurfers, sailboats and Aquacycles. The Red Eagle, a 40-passenger cruise boat, is docked at the marina, ready for daily scenic cruises around Flathead Lake. In the fall, the beautiful colors and numerous bald eagles along the shore of Flathead River can be seen.

A Western Town

Bigfork is a small community of 1,500 that capitalizes on its Western town appeal. Its history of Indian settlement, homesteading, steamships and logging has led to tourism. A short walk will take you from one end of Bigfork to the other, and you'll pass galleries, gift shops and restaurants with Western facades and made-in-Montana baskets, pottery, watercolor and oil paintings, marble, wood and bronze sculptures, clothing, jewelry, food and photos.

A variety of rental boats are available.

For 28 seasons, the Bigfork Playhouse has presented four American musicals Monday through Saturday from June through August. The crowds come from throughout the West and Canada to fill the historic theater to capacity throughout the summer.

The lure of Bigfork draws substantial numbers of summertime residents, and the population swells to 2,500, counting tourists. After the Christmas holidays, however, many businesses close until spring.

The Best Dining

Undoubtedly, the best year-round dining in Bigfork is at Marina Cay's Bay Club restaurant. Seating 125, the intimate tables are covered by pastel linens and topped with fresh flowers. You may choose the All-American or Continental breakfast, or opt for a Belgian waffle, French toast, buttermilk pancakes or an omelette. For lunch, there are gourmet hamburgers, a deli sandwich with fresh fruit or steak fries, the soup of the day or a fresh pasta. There is no dinner menu. The five to eight specialties are announced by the waiter who takes your order then promptly returns with a basket filled with hot, freshly baked bread. Marina Cay can also handle conventions and business meetings.

Getting There

From Polson, Montana, take Highway 35, which follows the east side of the lake, north into Bigfork. At the second flashing yellow light, turn right and follow the signs to Marina Cay. From the north, turn left at the Bigfork sign and Marina Cay will be on your right.

FLATHEAD LAKE LODGE

Address:	P.O. Box 248, Bigfork, MT 59911
Telephone:	(406) 837-4391
Location:	Highway 35, one mile south of Bigfork
Hosts:	Doug and Maureen Averill
Rates:	Adults $875, teenagers $693, children from four to 12 $595, children under four $96, single occupancy $890. Rates Sunday to Sunday
Credit Cards:	None. Personal checks accepted
Remarks:	No pets. Open May through September Reservations required

The Averill family's Flathead Lake Lodge and Dude Ranch offers guests one full week of lodging, meals and recreational activities on their 2,000-acre ranch on the east shore of Flathead Lake, and has been doing so since 1945. The lodge caters to families with children of all ages, and the 100 guests are limited only by their inability to do everything at once.

"People come here for the horses," says Doug Averill, an ex-rodeo rider who became manager of the ranch when his dad, Les Averill, retired in 1975. "We have dude horses for the inexperienced riders and quality quarterhorses for those who know how to handle that kind of horse. A lot of the people are simply nuts about horses." And so the Averills give them horses morning, noon and night. Guests can sign up for breakfast rides, group rides, and family rides or fast rides. The wranglers start their day at 5:30, but even at that hour there are kids down at the stable to help them brush and feed the horses.

Kids Rodeo

At the end of the week, there is a kid's rodeo, and children of all ages participate in the barrel races, pole bending contests, three-legged races and the water balloon challenge. "The rodeo is for fun. It's not meant to be competitive," Doug explains. Once a week, a roping club comes to the ranch to put on a performance, and Buck, a longtime ranch hand, entertains guests with stories and demonstrations of old-time skills such as braiding rope.

On Flathead Lake

As much as guests love the horses, it would be impossible to forget the lake. The clear blue waters of Flathead lap at the shore of the ranch, and guests are encouraged to take out the sailboats, fishing boats, canoes and windsurfers at any time. There's waterskiing everyday at one o'clock, and an experienced waterfront hand is nearby to handle the powerboat and give lessons.

For those who prefer the moving water of a river, Flathead Lake Lodge offers raft trips and inner tube floats on the Swan and Flathead rivers. For even more excitement, guests can go white water rafting or take a raft fishing trip.

The main lodge faces Flathead Lake.

If the horses and the lake don't take up all the free time a guest has, he or she can play tennis, volleyball or basketball, swim in the lake or pool, attend the nightly beach fires and sing-alongs, work in the ranch's vegetable and flower garden, take a day trip to Glacier National Park, or just sit on one of the dozens of benches, chairs or lounges that are spread around the ranch. The game room appeals to kids from three to 30, and a game room monitor takes kids on nature hikes to gather the raw materials for future projects: painted rock people and pinecone cowboys.

There are, in fact, only two things that guests can't do: they can't watch television and they can't play video games. There aren't any in the cabins or the lodges.

Family Style Dining

The Civilian Conservation Corps built the Main Lodge and the South Lodge in 1932, and both two-story Western structures have large lobbies with huge river rock fireplaces. The walls and floors are constructed of larch, and so are the tables and chairs. The Main Lodge houses the office, Saddle Sore Saloon (guests bring their own liquor), kitchen and family style dining room, a few rooms for single guests and quarters for the kitchen staff. The walls of the lobby are decorated with trophies of past hunting expeditions: bear, moose, elk, deer, bighorn sheep, antelope, mountain goat and buffalo. The 25 to 30 families that arrive at the ranch each Sunday are housed in 17 cottages and cabins, constructed in the 1940s and '50s, that accommodate four to six people. Each unit has its own bath, two or three bedrooms, a comfortable living room and Western furnishings. Other outbuildings contain the game room, laundry, wood shop and horses' tack room and stables.

Activities peak here three times a day.

The lodge and dude ranch are completely self-sustaining. The kitchen staff bakes the bread, plans the desserts and prepares all the meals. Breakfast might consist of huckleberry pancakes and bacon and eggs one day and omelettes the next. Coffee is always served first thing in the morning, for the Averills know that many adults enjoy that first cup while standing next to a crackling fire in the Main Lodge. Lunch is light: salads and quiche or the food that kids like — hamburgers and soups. If the weather cooperates, and it usually does in the summer, lunch is served outside on the deck overlooking the lake. Dinner might be a steak fry, fresh salmon, chicken, prime rib or a whole pig.

The unique combination of the lodge, its setting and recreational activities give the Averills an almost unheard-of repeat rate. Over 70 percent of Flathead Lake Lodge's guests come back again. Many come every other year, like one German family who has made the trip seven times. Mr. and Mrs. George Wood hold the record: they have come every summer for the last 37 years. It all started with their honeymoon... George and his wife have never missed the first two weeks of August on the lake since. George became known as Grandpa George and even gave Maureen Averill, Doug's wife, away on her wedding day. Like so many guests, George is family now.

Getting There

From Polson, follow Highway 35 north along the east side of Flathead Lake. The sign for the ranch is about one mile south of Bigfork. From Glacier National park, take Highway 40 toward Columbia Falls, turn onto 206, heading south. It will join with Highway 35, which will lead you past Bigfork and one mile south to the ranch.

MOUNTAIN SKY GUEST RANCH

Address:	Big Creek Road, Emigrant, MT, P.O. Box 1128, Bozeman, MT 59771 for reservations.
Telephone:	(406) 587-1244, toll free (800) 548-3392
Location:	Four and one-half miles up Big Creek Road, off Highway 89 in south central Montana
Host:	Alan Brutger
Rates:	July and August: Adult single $895, double $825. Children 7-12 $725, six and under $460. June, September and October: Adult single $805, double $742, children 7-12 $652, six and under $414.
Credit Cards:	None. Personal checks accepted
Remarks:	No pets. Open May to October.

Nestled high in the Rocky Mountains, just 30 miles from Yellowstone National Park, is Mountain Sky Guest Ranch, one of the top-rated guest ranches in the Northern Rockies.

Mountain Sky was built in the mid-1930s — the old cabins, the lodge and their furniture were crafted with wood taken right off the property — and operated until the 1950s as a dude ranch. In the years that followed, the ranch was bought and sold several times, and the buildings fell into disrepair. In 1980, Dan Brutger, a Minnesota contractor, purchased the 6,000-acre ranch, remodeled the old buildings and added new ones. His intention was to establish the premier guest ranch in Montana, one that offered memorable Western vacations for the entire family. The emphasis was then, and is now, on the family.

"Yellowstone City," the main lodge, has a massive rock fireplace, braided rugs over wooden floors and a piano, unlike any other, made from rough-hewn lodgepole pine. The lodge houses the kitchen, the lounge and full-service bar, the dining rooms and the office.

"Cinnebar," like all the new cabins, has a spacious sitting room, wall-to-wall carpeting, comfortable furniture, a small refrigerator, modern bath, generous closet space and a Montana-sized picture window that displays the surrounding mountains. The cabin sleeps two to four, and, most importantly, it is a place in which a family can feel at home.

"Black Pine" is an example of one of the old cabins that has been thoroughly remodeled to include modern conveniences without destroying the rustic ambiance. These one-, two- or three-bedroom cabins have a rock fireplace or wood burning stove and Western post-and-pole furniture, and can accommodate families large or small in comfort. All of the cabins at Mountain Sky, new and old, have daily housekeeping, an inviting front porch with hanging flower baskets, and a bowl of fresh fruit ready for incoming guests. Don't look for telephones or televisions in the cabins, because there aren't any.

There are plenty of places to relax in the warm central lounge.

Sunday to Sunday

The week at Mountain Sky begins on Sunday. Guests can use the afternoon to freshen up, unpack, walk down to the stables or tennis courts, go for a swim or get to know their neighbors. Mondays begin with a horse roundup, when the ranch wranglers assess each guest's riding skill before assigning him or her a horse for the week. On Monday night, there is a weekly ice-breaker softball game in which everyone is either player or cheerleader. By the time the game is over, everyone knows each other's name.

A Relaxed Structure

"Our dude ranch is for people who like horses," Brutger says. "But we don't push horses on people who don't care to ride. We have a relaxed structure at Mountain Sky. There's plenty to do here, but there's no timetable. People make their own choices."

For horse lovers there are morning, afternoon and dinner rides over hundreds of miles of riding trails on the ranch and adjacent Gallatin National Forest. Riders can spot deer, elk, moose, black bear and cougar amid the rocky cliffs, grassy meadows and forested slopes of the ranch. Guests can walk down to Big Creek to flyfish, or head for Armstrong or Nelson creeks, two Blue Ribbon trout streams nearby. There is also tennis on championship courts, volleyball, basketball or billiards.

The Basics of Horsemanship

Although this is a family-oriented ranch, Brutger and his staff know very well that parents need a vacation, too. For children, a highly qualified director

The historic barn and corrals are a short walk from the cabins.

supervises nature walks, swimming, games and fishing in a private trout pond. A Children's Wrangler gives guidance and instructions on horsemanship basics, while the chef prepares "Kids Meals." Adults are offered a variety of activities in the new "fun through fitness" program. These professionally taught classes specialize in individualized workouts, aerobic activity, stretching and relaxing. Other options include guided hikes and aquacize, the aquatic equivalent to aerobics.

Yellowstone National Park is about the only reason to leave Mountain Sky Ranch — its geysers, canyons, prairies, hot springs, lakes and wildlife are not to be missed. The park is a pleasurable day trip from the ranch. Picnic lunches and car pools are easily arranged.

Mountain air and activity works up mighty appetites, and the ranch is well equipped to meet the challenge. The pastries, cinnamon rolls and croissants are freshly baked each morning, and guests may order an omelette, ham and eggs, fresh fruits, or blueberry pancakes. Lunchtime offers a casual buffet, served outside, with a line-up of salads, soups and a hot specialty dish. Dinner is a gourmet affair with beef Wellington, poached salmon, veal medallion or rack of lamb.

Getting There

Turn off I-90 at Livingston, heading south on Highway 89. Thirty-nine miles south of Livingston (past Emigrant), you will see the sign for Mountain Sky Guest Ranch at the Big Creek Road turn off. Be advised that the four and one-half miles to the ranch are slow. For travelers headed to the ranch from Yellowstone, the Mountain Sky turn off will be on the left-hand side of Highway 89, 30 miles north of Gardiner.

OTHER HELPFUL BOOKS AND INFORMATION

During our travels we often spot other books that provide excellent information to increase the enjoyment of the area. Here is a list of some of those books, both pictorials and guides that we have found helpful.

Northern California

Napa Wine Country, by Earl Roberge. 172 color photographs and an excellent reference source on the region.

California, Its Coast and Desert, by Robert Reynolds, Ruth Kirk and Archie Satterfield. 200 color photographs covering the coastal region and the desert.

Travel Guide to Northern California, by Sunset Book Company. In 128 pages the editors do their normal wonderful job of providing enough useful information to make every trip memorable.

Oregon

Oregon Coast, by Ray Atkeson and Archie Satterfield. 119 color photos to explore the entire coast.

Oregon II, by Ray Atkeson and Archie Satterfield. 200 color photographs of the entire state.

Northwest Wine Country, by Ron and Glenda Holden. A very handy pocketbook-size guide to the growing wine country. It contains maps and all the necessary details.

Travel Guide to Oregon, by Sunset Book Company. Another 128-page step-by-step winner to the enjoyment of the entire state.

Washington

Seattle, by Charles Krebs and Timothy Egan. Another beautifully printed hardbound edition using 110 color photos and text to explore the Northwest's largest and most spectacular city.

Mount St. Helens - A Changing Landscape, by Chuck Williams. This book covers the mountain before and after the great eruption, as seen through the eyes of 50 photographers, from the turn of the century to the present. 85 color and 409 black and white photos tell the story.

The Tastes of Washington, by Fred Brack and Tina Bell. A spectacular new cookbook with color photography that features the selection and enjoyment of Northwest foods.

Travel Guide to Washington, by Sunset Book Company. Another guide not to be missed from the "granddaddy" of guide book companies.

Idaho

Idaho, by John Marshall and Cort Conley. A colorful photogenic essay portrays the state from the forested northern panhandle to the sagebrush of the south.

Idaho for the Curious, by Cort Conley. A unique 704-page paperback that provides incredibly detailed information on the history and sights accessible by passenger car along the 14,000 miles of Idaho roads.

Montana

Montana Wilderness: Discovering the Heritage, by Steve Woodruff and Don Schwennesen. A well done, 116-page exploration of the state.

We have found that Bill and Pam Bryan from Bozeman offer an excellent service planning personalized travel and vacation plans throughout the Rockies. They do an outstanding job of matching your travel wishes with the hidden places they have found.

Their company is called:

Off the Beaten Path
109 East Main St.
Bozeman, Montana 59715

NOTES

NOTES

NOTES

TO REORDER

If you would like to re-order additional copies of *Special Places*, please use the attached mailing card. If the card has already been used, send your name, address and $13.95 plus $1.50 for postage and handling to:

Graphic Arts Publishing Co.
P.O. Box 10306
Portland, Oregon 97210

In addition to Special Places, Graphic Arts publishes about 50 other books ranging from Alaska to New England. If you would like an annual catalog and price sheet they would be pleased to include one when you request.

PLEASE HELP!

Your reactions to the Special Places in this book are very important to us. Please complete one of the attached post cards after you experience one of the Special Places. We will use the information you provide to help us in the on-going process of monitoring the quality and service of each Special Place.

Something for You

Each time you send in a postcard (or a letter if you choose) we will enter your name in a Quarterly drawing. One prize will be awarded in each of four random drawings in January, April, July, and October. The prize will be two nights lodging in the Special Place of your choice. To be eligible, entrants must be 21 years of age.

Travel News Quarterly

We also publish a free quarterly newsletter, featuring events and activities happening at and around the Special Places. Newly discovered Special Places are previewed prior to publishing of the next book. If you would like to be on the list to receive the Travel News Quarterly, please check the box on the postcard.

Other Places You Feel are Special

If during your travels you discover a place you feel is quite special, we would appreciate you letting us know. Any suggestions in the 13 western states and two western Canadian provinces will be investigated.

Thanks
Fred and Mardi

Special Places

for the discerning traveler

Please send me _____ copies of SPECIAL PLACES® at 13.95 each, plus $1.50 for shipping and handling. Send to:

_____
NAME

_____
ADDRESS

_____
CITY

_____
STATE   ZIP

In

NORTHERN CALIFORNIA, OREGON

WASHINGTON, BRITISH COLUMBIA

IDAHO AND MONTANA

Special Places

Dear Fred and Mardi,

We experienced the following Special Place: _____

_____ on _____ (Reservation date)

and have these comments: _____

_____

_____

Free Drawing

Please enter me in the free quarterly drawing

_____
Name

_____
Address   City   State/Zip

I would ☐, I would not ☐, like to receive the free TRAVEL-NEWS QUARTERLY on the Special Places.

New Discoveries

We discovered a place we feel is Special and think you should see:

_____

_____

Graphic Arts Center Publishing Company
P.O. Box 10306
Portland, Oregon 97210

Special Places
P.O. Box 378
Issaquah, WA 98027

Special Places

for the discerning traveler

Please send me _____ copies of SPECIAL PLACES®
at 13.95 each, plus $1.50 for shipping and handling. Send to:

_____
NAME

_____
ADDRESS

_____
CITY

_____
STATE   ZIP

In

NORTHERN CALIFORNIA, OREGON

WASHINGTON, BRITISH COLUMBIA

IDAHO AND MONTANA

Special Places

Dear Fred and Mardi,
We experienced the following Special Place: _____
_____ on _____ (Reservation date)
and have these comments: _____
_____
_____

Free Drawing
Please enter me in the free quarterly drawing

_____
Name

_____
Address   City   State/Zip

I would ☐, I would not ☐, like to receive the free TRAVEL-NEWS
QUARTERLY on the Special Places.

New Discoveries
We discovered a place we feel is Special and think you should see:

_____
_____

Graphic Arts Center Publishing Company
P.O. Box 10306
Portland, Oregon 97210

P.O. Box 378
Issaquah, WA 98027